ELY'S 'MIDGE' GREEN

THE STORY OF A SIX-FOOT-FOUR CENTRE FORWARD

IN A FIVE-FOOT-NINE BODY

By

Steve Green

Published by New Generation Publishing in 2016

Copyright © Steve Green 2016

First Edition

The author asserts the moral right under the Copyright, Designs and Patents Act 1988 to be identified as the author of this work.

All Rights reserved. No part of this publication may be reproduced, stored in a retrieval system or transmitted, in any form or by any means without the prior consent of the author, nor be otherwise circulated in any form of binding or cover other than that which it is published and without a similar condition being imposed on the subsequent purchaser.

www.newgeneration-publishing.com

New Generation Publishing

PROLOGUE

So why – as the proverbial non-celebrity – did I write this book? That is a question I have frequently been asked by family and friends in recent times! It is certainly not to 'celebrate' my 'achievements' in the world of football, which it could reasonably be argued amounted to comparatively FA in the grand scheme of things (and I have always regretted the fact that there is no edition of the Rothmans Football Yearbook that contains my name – not even as 'A Trialist' which the Scottish Football Association sometimes uses to identify certain anonymous goal scorers in their League records).

It was simply that I decided I wanted to get everything down on paper, and see how it turned out. I have been positively encouraged to do so by some people, and positively discouraged by others who quite reasonably consider that unless you are a 'celebrity', no-one will be remotely interested in your life – particularly inasmuch as it revolves around the game of football. They may well be right, but I went ahead anyway, and to be honest found the whole experience intensely rewarding. I recalled things that had happened and things that people had said, which I didn't even know I had forgotten in the first place!

My good friend and 'proof-reader' Linda suggested that I should summarise – in essence – what football has meant to me and what it means to me now. As usual, she was right, so here goes.

Friendship. I made more friends – including team-mates, opponents, officials, club members, fans – than I could ever recount. I thank them all.

Memories. If not for football, I'm sure my life would not contain anywhere near as many worthwhile recollections.

Pride. I am so proud of what I achieved, despite some regrets which will become apparent (if of course, you can be arsed to read on...)

Excitement. I found everything about my life in football so exciting. OK, so I need therapy, but there you have it. I loved it and I still love it!

Strength. Both physical and character-wise. Football motivated me to become physically strong, and it also helped to develop my character. It helped me understand what it means to have integrity and it encouraged me to be (relatively) honest. One of the things I hate about the modern game is the lack of integrity and honesty. Diving, appealing, shirt-pulling, cheating. (I have pulled shirts in the past, but not in a sneaky way. It was always blatantly obvious, depending on how far my opponent's shirt would stretch).

Bravery. I could be wrong, but I think I was one of the bravest players around. I really didn't give enough consideration to my own well-being at times. 'The Moron' can testify to that (see *Chapter Seventeen – 'Manny'*).

Self-improvement. Football shaped my life. I improved (at least initially), and even at the age of 55 I can still hold my own with the youngsters. (If they tell you differently, don't listen to them. They are probably drunk).

Geography. Yes, I know that's a bit of a shock, but it's true! Through football, I know more about geography than I could ever have known otherwise! I even know where Tamworth is!

Finally, I appreciate that some of the things in this book may appear rather self-congratulatory, but although the book is (obviously) about me, I felt it was necessary to describe events as if from an observer's point of view. For example, if I scored what I would have considered to be a 'spectacular' goal if I had seen it scored by someone else, then I have described it as 'spectacular'. Otherwise, simply stating the fact that I scored, over and over again, would have made pretty dull reading (or duller, at least).

I should also point out that there are a lot of football scores in this book. But much like the classified football results on a Saturday, these are not included on the basis that they constitute 'interesting narrative'. They are included for the sake of completeness alone, so I would recommend that readers – who, unlike me, might care little about statistical background – gloss over such detail without the slightest twinge of guilt.

So here it is. If no-one ever reads it, no harm done. If someone reads it and hates it, so what? If someone reads it and actually enjoys it, so much the better.

CHAPTER ONE: Why 'Midge'?

Many moons ago during my days at St Mary's Junior School in Ely, 'play-time' was much less virtual than the advent of technology has made it nowadays. I had never heard of computers, let alone *Football Manager* and *FIFA*. So in the playground, we actually played (in the absence of a ball) with a lump of 'coke' from the large pile of black rock that fuelled the school boilers, and 'conkers' was played (in the absence of a nearby horse chestnut tree) with the huge leaves from a maple tree which grew near the boundary wall.

Health and Safety pedants nowadays would no doubt approve (heartily, and in triplicate) of the fact that shards of conkers were not flying around to blind, maim and decapitate unsuspecting schoolchildren in the vicinity. The booting of rock hard lumps of 'coke' around the playground on the other hand, would undoubtedly have had the H & S brigade reaching for their self-administered defibrillators, and the Council would probably have instigated rabid campaigns for the school to be closed down whilst solid fuel fragments were extracted from the eye sockets and ear drums of innocent bystanders.

My mum however, was more concerned about the detrimental effect it had on my shoes.

It was during one such 'coke'-kicking session that I acquired the nickname that has remained with me ever since. Darren Fincham – possibly the tallest boy in the known universe as well as our school – was a bit strange at times, to say the least. As I dribbled the 'coke' past him (possibly running between his legs due to the stark difference in our respective inches above sea-level), he suddenly started squealing "Midgeville! Midgeville!" The first half of that name stuck instantly, and I have to say it was infinitely preferable to the unimaginative 'Greeny' which I had been lumbered with for the previous six or seven years since birth. (My cousin Dale was labelled with the equally banal nickname of 'Beany', after the common vegetable).

Many years later some of the players at Ely City FC labelled me 'Sniffer', but thankfully this was more connected with my predatory instincts in front of goal rather than any dog-like predilection for inhaling the scent of any bitches I happened to fancy (or at least I think that was the reason).

My first experience of properly organised football was for the St Mary's School team, where – as a third-year pupil – I played right-back for a team predominantly made up of fourth-years. The following season I moved to centre-half, in our usual 2-3-5 formation, still wearing a pair of hob-nail football boots that my uncle 'Mossy' had worn playing for Littleport Town in the 1950s.

The school team manager went by the name of Bill Barnett, a West Bromwich Albion supporter who drove a navy blue Volkswagen Beetle which had its engine in the boot. Whenever he lifted up the bonnet of his car, I always thought he was about to check the oil or something, but instead he always came out with an orange net containing two laced brown leather footballs.

The school team colours were blue and white striped shirts with white shorts and white socks, which were of course West Bromwich Albion's colours! In 1968, West Brom reached the FA Cup Final and Everton were the opposition. Everyone at school seemed to want West Brom to win (probably due to threats of grievous bodily harm from Bill Barnett if they did otherwise!), so I plumped instead for the 'Toffees' and have followed them ever since. My newly-acquired team did of course, lose 1-0 to a goal from the late England striker Jeff Astle.

Our school team shirts were made of a material which would have been more at home on a heavy duty deckchair, and which absorbed water like the most efficient sponge known to man. When it rained you not only looked like a wet deckchair, but it felt as if some stranger was still asleep in the chair on top of you.

Bill frequently described me as "the smallest centre-half in the world", and I doubt that he was far wrong as anyone wishing to challenge me for the title of 'most diminutive number five on the planet' would almost certainly have been too young to be considered in the first place. Yes, I was that small. Nevertheless, I learned to jump and head soggy wet lumps of leather several yards at a time. Later on in my career, I learned to head the lighter balls even further, and sometimes a net was even required to stop them trundling into the ditch behind the goal!

I don't remember any school matches as a third-year full-back, but as a fourth-year centre-half in the Rumpelstiltskin* mould I recall that we were unbeaten at home. We lost only two matches all season – 8-2(!) at Burrowmoor (March) and 6-1(!) at Chatteris, but managed to hold those opponents 2-2 and 1-1 at home. My mate Jonathan Peacock scored most of our goals, but he was nearly as tall as Darren Fincham and it counted for a lot at that age.

> *Bill – who was the Music Teacher as well as the PE Teacher – called me into the school dining room one afternoon. He was sitting at the piano and when I arrived he started to play one particular note continually, albeit with a varied rhythm. I started to feel quite scared when he began to speak in time with that rhythm.*
>
> *"Here..come..I,*
> *The..land..to..spy,*

To-find-out-all-I-can!
To..steal..to..rob,
To..do..a..dirty..job,
Let-in-this-little-man, that's-me!
Let-in-this-little-man!
Through..the..window..I..can..squeeeeze!
When..doors..are..locked..I..pass..with..eeease!"

Bill eventually explained that he wanted me to play the part of Rumpelstiltskin in a musical production that the school was putting on. I was in the school choir so he knew that I had a good singing voice, but no doubt my vertically-challenged stature helped to persuade him that I was eminently more suited to the role than say, my school chum Darren Fincham. When I politely declined his 'offer', he explained to me in no uncertain terms that my school footballing days were over unless I complied with his request. The fact that I can still remember many of the lyrics over 40 years later indicates how hard we subsequently rehearsed for that show!

Although I was so small that the West Brom shirt made me look like a stripy, stumpy version of Rip Van Winkle (minus the hat), I managed to score my only goal of the 1970/1971 season from close range in a 3-0 win at Haddenham. It would be several years before I converted to a striker and found the net again at secondary school playing for one of the most unsuccessful school teams in modern history (because despite having the nucleus of the Ely Crusaders team in our line-up, we didn't manage to win a single game until the fourth year!)

My first ever medal came in the shape of County Schools recognition in 1971, albeit as a substitute. I had picked up a knee injury in the aforementioned game at Haddenham, so didn't make the starting line-up for the Cambridgeshire Schools Team. I was nevertheless immensely proud, having struck a sporting blow for midgets all over the globe.

The final medal of my competitive career came around 35 years later when my Sunday team Ely Park Rangers lost 1-0 to FC Sterling in the final of the 2002/2003 Cambs FA Millennium Cup. Appropriately perhaps, that tie – the last Sunday match of my career – was played at Julius Martin Lane, the home of one of my previous Saturday clubs Soham Town Rangers.

At the start of the following 2003/2004 Sunday League season I made it clear – as I always did – that I did not want to be involved in either pre-season training or friendly matches for Ely Park Rangers, having participated in neither for many years. (In my experience more people are injured in training or in friendlies than at any other time. Oh, and I hated training). I always appreciated that this could (initially at least) cost me my place in the team, but I was happy to be substitute for either the first team or the Reserves (and as a qualified referee, I was probably made for running the line).

When the season got underway however, I received no contact from the club at all. I therefore made the decision to retire from football at the age of 43. The club player-manager, Gary Dewsbury, did get in touch a few weeks later, but I had made up my mind that my role as a central defender – the position to which I had reverted in my dotage – would be reprised no more.

I knew I would miss the 'craic', but by this time I was living in Gamlingay anyway, so decided that the one thing I definitely wouldn't miss was the 75-mile or so round trip every Sunday to Ely – the city where I was born and had lived for more than 40 years of my life.

I was still writing the weekly Junior Football column for the Ely Standard newspaper at that time, so when I spoke to local team managers on the telephone there were frequent attempts to tempt me out of retirement. They were unsuccessful however; I had decided to quit when my body was still (relatively) intact from an injury point of view, and no-one managed to change my mind.

After moving to Gamlingay to live with my partner (now my wife) Denise and her two children Jordan and Nathan, we had our first family holiday together in Rhodes. Shortly after arriving at the hotel, I discovered that a football tournament was taking place at 4.00 pm that afternoon, so I decided to go along and unsurprisingly found that I was probably the oldest one there. Four captains were selected and picked their players one-by-one, and naturally enough the short, balding, slightly overweight Elian* was one of the last to be selected. I reflected on the irony that if this situation had occurred many years ago in the playground at school, I would have been one of the first to be picked.

> *Elians are natives of Ely in Cambridgeshire. Littleportians are natives of nearby Littleport in the same county. I kid you not.*

Despite my involvement, our team in Rhodes had the youngest average age, and that was undoubtedly a 'plus' in the searing afternoon heat. I managed to score early on in our semi-final, but we soon found ourselves 3-1 down before recovering to draw and then win the match in a penalty shoot-out. I was already feeling knackered by this stage, with the words 'retirement', 'stupid old fool' and 'coronary' circling like grinning vultures inside my red, boiling head.

The other finalists fancied their chances against our rag-tag bunch of misfits, and I recall that they had the proverbial 'brick shit-house' in their team, covered in tattoos and going by the name of 'Rico', a name which he presumably had emblazoned on his arms so that when he awoke each morning, he could remember who he was.

The match was scoreless when the ball broke between 'Rico' and myself, but I never cared how big my opponents were and I wasn't going to pull out of the tackle. To my surprise however, 'Rico' did, presumably because he thought that I would be the one to duck out. I was therefore able to lift the ball over his foot, beat two players and then steer the ball into the path of our 'captain', who rounded the goalkeeper and slotted home from the narrowest of angles. As I walked back to my own half, 'Rico' came up to me and said: "Next time I won't take it easy on you. I'll go right through you and break your leg." Yeah, right.

'Rico' stormed off at the finish and was left to console himself with thoughts of what unpleasant injuries he should have inflicted on me at the start of my holiday, his team having failed to recover the 1-0 deficit. Nice bloke.

Our next two summer holidays were at a place called Sissi Bay on the north coast of Crete. There was an artificially turfed six-a-side pitch on the edge of the complex, so I played on a regular basis there. It was mostly good-natured stuff, although there was one lad called Adam – who apparently lived with his parents nearby, as opposed to being a holiday-maker – who could best be described as 'gobby'. He had the particularly annoying habit of providing a running commentary on his own performance during the game, which made him a bit of a target for – ahem – infringements.

A couple of years later, at the tender age of 46, I was compiling my football column for the Ely Standard newspaper as usual on a Monday night and was chatting with the then Sports Editor, who was also called Adam funnily enough. He was playing for Cambs League Division 1B side Tuddenham Rovers, a team based in Suffolk which was managed by a former Ely City and Soham Town Rangers team-mate of mine, Colin Anderson.

Tuddenham – who a few years earlier had attempted to buy their way to the Cambs Premier League title and Jewson League football – were top of Division 1B in 2005/2006, but had been forced to forfeit three points, having postponed a *home* fixture due to a lack of players. I said to Adam that he should have telephoned me, because if nothing else I could have stood on the wing as 'nuisance-value' and panted vigorously every time I moved. This would be bound to distract the opposition, as they would be under the impression that a coronary seizure was imminent.

Eventually my opportunity to self-combust arrived, because Rovers were short for the visit to Gransden Chequers – a club based conveniently only three miles from my Gamlingay home. A few minutes after the start of the game I was breathing out of places with no proximity to the lungs, but didn't think I was doing too badly for someone whose playing days belonged to the era of music hall.

I did clip the bar with a tame effort from just outside the penalty area in the first half, but we were eventually beaten 2-1 by a poor side. Just before the end of the game, one of the Gransden midfielders ran past me and deliberately flashed his elbow into my midriff. I responded with a few choice words, to which he replied: "What's up 'pops'?" This came as something of a shock to me. In my mind's eye, I was a lithe, gifted teenager coming back from a career-threatening injury. In the eyes of everyone else however, I was a balding, rotund pensioner, better equipped for pitch-rolling than rolling back the years on the pitch.

However, I was now bitten by the most lethal bug known

to mankind; the 'play-once-a-year-despite-not-exercising-regularly-and-take-two-weeks-to-recover-after-making-a-complete-arse-of-oneself' bug.

About eight months later (when I may have still been feeling the after-effects of the titanic tussle between Gransden Chequers and Tuddenham Rovers), I was asked to play in a representative cup match for Peterborough Taxes. The interest amongst East Anglian Revenue & Customs offices was so great that a grand total of two teams entered the competition, so we were in the final!

The fixture took place at Cornard United's ground, and we were facing the holders – a bunch of young footballers who knew how to play a bit. The fact that there were at least three players in our line-up older than me tells you everything you need to know about the profile of our motley crew of geriatrics. The referee blew the whistle to signal the start of the 'match' (for want of a better term), and when (hypothetically speaking) he glanced at his watch 20 minutes later we were already four goals down.

Losing I can cope with, having pretty much perfected the art during my football career. What I have never been able to abide is my marker continually 'touching' me, which I have always regarded as a sign of homosexuality. Being 'fingered' (from behind) by an individual who perhaps used to live in a closet held no appeal for me.

So the first time he touched me, I knocked his hand away. The second time, I suggested he should undertake some sexy travel (but not with me). On the third occasion, I informed him that I would inflict some bodily harm on him if he did not desist. For a while he kept his distance, but as we started to improve following a brilliant free-kick from Ronnie Fortune which reduced the deficit to 4-1, he started to take his rather offensive defensive responsibilities too seriously again.

One further verbal warning did not have the desired effect, so with seconds remaining and – remarkably – with the score still standing at 4-1, I chased him towards his own penalty area. It was over in a flash. I clipped his heels causing him to fall forward, and as his body slumped to the turf I ran along his back without breaking stride. The referee's whistle sounded (not for a free-kick, but for the end of the match), upon which the perforated defender immediately squared up to me. "What was all that about?" he squealed. "I did warn you", I sighed, and trudged off to the dressing room to start my recuperation.

This in turn reminds me of an incident some years earlier, often re-told over open camp fires by my ex-football colleagues in HM Revenue & Customs, Cambridge.

We (Cambridge Taxes) were playing at Ipswich, and I was playing in defence, shepherding the ball back to emergency goalkeeper Kevin Crouch. The opponent behind me (a lanky streak of piss with ginger hair) was unable to get to the ball because of my gargantuan torso, so he thrust his right arm underneath my armpit and punched me in the eye socket. He must have thought that this blind-side assault would leave him an unhindered path to goal, but within a fraction of a second his nose – as he knew it – was a distant memory.

As the loose ball trundled into the goalkeeper's arms, the referee ran up and asked me what had happened. "Well," I said, as the fleshy material around my swollen eye turned several shades of purple, "he punched me in the eye so I broke his nose".

"Oh," said the referee, and play continued.

I suppose we should both have been sent off (it would have been the only dismissal of my entire career), but my reaction was instinctive whereas his action was premeditated. Justice in my opinion, was served. His nose in my opinion, was now flat.

Although never red-carded, I did once have a caution upgraded by the Cambs FA and served a month's suspension as a result. Playing for Ely City Reserves at Milton, I got involved in an ongoing physical spat with the home side's left back called Nicky. Before long we were tangling on the floor like a couple of street urchins, which earned cautions for us both. The referee's report however, indicated that I had thrown a punch, so the caution was upgraded to a dismissal. I appealed and contacted Nicky who despite our differences was quite happy to provide a written statement confirming that no punch was thrown.

I subsequently contacted the Ely City club secretary Derek Oakey to find out what had happened at the appeal hearing, only to be informed that he hadn't even bothered sending the letter to the FA because he didn't think it was worth it! With the exception of a subsequent (failed) attempt to break into Ely City's first team, I never played for the 'Robins' again. I never rubbed along very well with Mr Oakey. I thought he was a buffoon.

Many years later, when I was covering the whole of the Ely Standard Sports Editor's job and was therefore writing weekly articles about the likes of Ely City FC, he rang me to complain about something I had written (or more likely, had not written) in the previous week's edition. Needless to say, we did not see eye-to-eye on the matter. He then had the temerity to say "My father always taught me that if a job's worth doing, it's worth doing well". That's right, Mr Oakey, but weren't you the bloke that:

a) Earned me a suspension and a fine simply by not bothering to post a letter?
b) Got my team Ely City Reserves kicked out of the Creake Shield semi-final for failing to submit the

legitimate signing-on form for Andy Day who played in the 4-1 quarter-final win at Cambridge University Press?

Maybe he had some sort of allergy to postage stamp adhesive...

I appreciate that some of this vitriolic comment might make it appear as if I am some sort of pocket-sized psychopath, but most footballers (and indeed sportsmen as a whole) will tell you that the persona you adopt in certain situations may be (and often is) totally at odds with your day-to-day behaviours.

I once read about something called 'The Games Theory', and it suggested that games were a good thing for individuals to undertake (either alone or in teams) because those games – whatever they happened to be – were played within a framework of rules, involved competition and resulted in an outcome (winning, losing, drawing). In other words, 'life' could effectively be encapsulated within the 'game', and as such enabled one to learn about 'life'.

Certainly, as a victim of bullying at school, sport gave me confidence and (most importantly) taught me how to look after myself – on the field and in my day-to-day existence, particularly at work where rules, competition and outcomes were and still are of vital importance.

My approach to both sport and life took a dramatic turn for the better in the 1975/76 season, at the age of 15, during the period I shall describe (perhaps ridiculously) as the 'Crusades'.

CHAPTER TWO: The Start of the 'Crusades'

Nowadays, kids seem to start playing organised football (in front of frequently over-zealous and at times, rabid parents) as soon as they learn to walk, but it wasn't like that in my time. You were forbidden by the school to play football outside that organised by the school until the age of 12. So it was at under-14 level that my career with Ely Crusaders FC finally got underway.

'Midge' Green still cut a diminutive figure at this age, whereas the (tragically suicidal) Len Alsop – All-England Hammer-Throwing Champion for his age and an imposing centre-half – already stood more than a foot taller than me. Consequently – despite being recognised at school as one of the best players in my age group – I could not command a regular place in Brian Atkin's Ely Crusaders line-up. I felt I should have been selected on merit, but frequently found myself sidelined for Colts League games whilst technically inferior, but taller boys from Ely and the surrounding villages pulled on the claret and sky blue colours of Crusaders instead.

We played our home games at 'Paradise', a large park ground in the centre of Ely which at the time housed Ely City Football Club, Ely Rugby Club, Ely Cricket Club, Ely Tennis Club and Ely Bowls Club. Our pitch was located on the Lynn Road side of the ground, and Ely City FC played on the main pitch which was next to New Barns Road on the other side of the rugby pitch and cricket square, but several years later they were forced to move to Downham Road on the outskirts of the city – evicting resident Sunday clubs Ely Crusaders and Ely Park Rangers – owing to the fact that they were not allowed to erect floodlights in the city centre. Crusaders therefore found themselves returning to their original home of 'Paradise' – albeit on Ely City's 'old' pitch – after City had replaced them at Downham Road, and Crusaders were joined at the venue by Ely rivals Park Rangers, who also relocated from Downham Road.

Ely Crusaders under-14s travelled to away games in a 'converted' navy blue Bedford van driven by Ian Smith's dad Ray Smith. When I say 'converted', I mean that the back of the van was empty, apart from four crates and two planks which provided seating for the players along either side. Again, it is not difficult to envisage what modern Health & Safety officials would make of those arrangements, as unfettered children rattled around like peppercorns in an empty locomotive soup can. Ray's son Ian was a gifted left-side midfielder who became one of my best friends, and who also scored with the greatest left-foot shot I ever saw (described in *Chapter Eleven – The FA Cups*).

One of my earliest recollections with Ely Crusaders under-14s (apart from a 12-0 drubbing by the Jerry Hutton-inspired Cambridge Hornets) was a two-legged cup match against Newmarket-based Hawthorns, who beat us 3-1 at home in the first leg. I came on as a late substitute in that match and struck the bar with virtually my first touch, so I was in the starting XI for the second leg, although we soon found ourselves 4-1 down on aggregate.

Midway through the first half however, a left wing cross arrowed towards me as I approached the penalty spot. I launched myself forward to score with a diving header, and that proved the catalyst for an incredible come-back – one of the many I would enjoy with Crusaders over the years. We subsequently scored four unanswered goals in the second period to run out 6-4 winners overall.

Still without a regular place in the starting line-up for league games, I was selected to play in a home friendly at 'Paradise'. Manager Brian Atkin informed me before the game that if I scored four goals, I would be chosen to play the following week. At half-time, with four goals already under my belt, I reminded Brian of his earlier promise. He informed me however, that I had not heard him correctly and actually needed 14 goals to secure my place! Sure enough, I was back on the substitute bench the following Sunday.

Despite my continuing frustrations at not being able to command a regular place in the side, the 1973/1974 Colts League campaign was nevertheless an interesting one. This was the season when we began our arch-rivalry with Brian Manning's Newmarket Valley side, and in this particular season we were to play them no less than six times.

There were only six teams in the under-14 league that season – Cambridge Crusaders, Cambridge Hornets, Newmarket Valley, Stretham Swifts, Wilbraham and ourselves. Stretham and Wilbraham were no-hopers, so it was left to the other four teams to contest the honours. The campaign began with the League Cup, and we were drawn in Group One alongside Cambridge Crusaders and Newmarket Valley. We finished comfortably bottom of the group, losing 5-1 at home and 6-2 away to our Cambridge namesakes, and 2-0 at home and 2-1 away to our Suffolk rivals. Four goals scored and 15 conceded in those four matches did not suggest a challenge for honours was likely, but when the league campaign got under way it was a different story altogether.

After thrashing Valley 4-0 in the opener and beating Wilbraham 3-0 away, we managed to draw 2-2 at home to Cambridge Crusaders. The two goals we conceded on that day proved to be the only ones we shipped in the first eight league fixtures, during which time we scored no less than 40. So going into our penultimate game at Newmarket, we only needed one point to clinch the championship. Valley did manage to breach our defence once, but we scored twice and the title was ours – much to the chagrin of Cambridge Crusaders, who were waiting for us in the final league game. As it was they ended our unbeaten league run by handing us a 6-2 beating for the second time that season, but it didn't matter.

In the Knock-out Cup we produced another stirring comeback after we flopped 3-0 at Cambridge Hornets in the semi-final first leg. They extended their advantage in the second leg, but we then scored five unanswered goals for a dramatic 5-4 aggregate win.

Before dealing with the subsequent Knock-out Cup Final encounter with Newmarket Valley, I feel it is worth mentioning that we did at last get the better of Cambridge Crusaders in the final of the Cambridge Hornets Invitation Cup, having dispatched Valley 3-2 away and Stretham 8-0 in the earlier rounds of the competition. Twice coming from a goal down to win that final 3-2 after extra-time, I can remember scoring our first with a shot off the underside of the bar. The fact that this is the only goal I can specifically recall scoring in the 1973/1974 season perhaps reflects how peripheral I was to the starting line-up each week.

I was however, in the side for the under-14 Knock-out Cup Final against Newmarket Valley. For the record we were soundly beaten 5-2, having trailed 4-1 at the break. What I consider may be of more interest perhaps, is a comparison between the two squads for that match, and the two squads which squared up for the Sunday League Cup Final nine years later, when the players had become adults.

In 1973/1974, Valley's squad included Nigel Fussey, Tony Marshall, Steve Kearns, Gary Davey and David Stanbridge. The Crusaders line-up included Roger Smith, Ian Smith, Marcus Humphry, Gary Chilvers, Steve Atkin and myself. Remarkably, those same 11 players were present once again in the final that took place between the sides nearly a decade later, and one of the linesmen – Terry Willson – held the flag for both ties as well! The outcome was unfortunately pretty much the same too with Crusaders narrowly losing out in a seven-goal thriller, but there is rather more to the story than that and I will come to that very shortly.

Returning to the 1982/1983 season, I had by that time firmly established myself in the Great Britain & Northern Ireland representative side for the Inland Revenue, otherwise known as the Inland Revenue Football Club. I had made my debut in the 1979/1980 season, scoring five times in a 16-0 demolition of the hapless Royal Courts of Justice.

The GB & NI representative side did not play in a league. It played in a single knock-out competition each season which was called the Lewis Cup, and it took the Inland Revenue Football Club 56 years to win it for the first time. That was in 1977/1978, when a predominantly Scottish side – including former Leeds United, Ipswich Town and Everton striker Rod Belfitt – lifted the trophy. Other ex-professionals in that side included Mervyn Jones (Hibernian), Lindsay Hamilton (Alloa Athletic), Alan Guild (East Fife, Cambridge United and Luton Town) and Billy McLaren (who played for eight Scottish League Clubs, including Hibernian, Partick Thistle and Queen of the South). With the exception of Belfitt – who was 15 years my senior and who effectively I 'replaced' in the side – I had the great honour of playing with them all. As for Belfitt, how could I 'replace' him? He may have been something of a journeyman striker, but he nevertheless scored 33 goals in 128 First Division appearances for Leeds.

By the time the 1982/1983 campaign got underway, I had

managed 11 Lewis Cup goals in as many appearances, but we had progressed no further than the semi-finals. In this particular season however, with Manchester-based John Heapy at the helm, I was perhaps in the form of my life.

After scoring once in the 5-1 win against Southend Civil Service, I was on target twice in the 4-1 victory over tough opponents MOD (Main). Both shots were unstoppable, and both were with my left foot – one in the top left-hand corner after a partially cleared corner, and one which pinged in low off the goalkeeper's left-hand post when it looked as if my run past two defenders had taken me so wide that such a finish looked improbable.

In the last eight of the competition I had my first encounter with the mighty Merseyside Civil Service, but with speedy Eastern Counties colleague John Wilson alongside me, we fairly ripped them apart. The first goal ballooned into the net off my backside as I slid in trying to kick it, but my second was a sharp turn and left-foot drive into the bottom corner after the ball had run across the front of my body with my back to goal, just inside the penalty area.

So Merseyside Civil Service were dispatched 5-2, and that left only DTI (Department of Trade & Industry) Phoenix Rovers in our way for a place in the Lewis Cup Final. It was a tough encounter, and at half-time the score was still 0-0. Then something quite remarkable happened. Sportsmen often talk about "being in the zone", and I don't know if that is a real sensation or not. If it is, then perhaps this was my time in that most special of places.

At the start of the second half, there was a melee in the centre circle, with two defenders and one of our players tussling for the ball. The DTI Phoenix sweeper was involved, and he was quite a clever player, but suddenly it was as if I could read his mind. What he was about to do – knock the ball back into his own half around the outside of the other players before circling back behind them to pass unhindered to the goalkeeper – would, in any other circumstances, have brilliantly cleared up the mess. But somehow I had read it, so when he played the ball backwards about 10 yards I was already running into its path.

He raced back desperately and was alongside me when I reached the edge of the penalty area, so I decided that this was the only opportunity I would have for a shot on goal. When I connected with the ball, I hit it in such a way that it felt to me as if it would soar about 30 yards over the bar. I mention this because normally when you hit a shot you have a 'feel' for where it is going. On this occasion however, it felt to me as if the ball would clear three sets of goalposts balanced one on top of the other, let alone one set. The next thing I knew however, was that the ball had looped over the advancing goalkeeper and had crashed into the middle of the net just underneath the crossbar for the opening goal. It must have looked a lot better than it felt, that's all I can say!

You could practically hear the air hissing out of the DTI inner-tubes after that. Soon afterwards, winger Paul Burke broke down the right and clipped a cross towards me on the penalty spot. I had made a run into the box but the ball was falling behind me, so I leaned back and somehow powered a header into the opposite left-hand corner. After the match, John Heapy said to me that I "must have a neck like a giraffe!" Anyone who has ever seen me however, will know that this comment was ridiculous; I might have a powerful (18-inch collar) neck, but to the casual observer it might appear that I have no neck at all.

Burke then dribbled his way once more down the right, and again his cross – with a slightly lower trajectory this time – was slightly behind me, so I flicked my right foot up at the back and managed to steer the ball into the right-hand corner, totalling wrong-footing the 'keeper. So after struggling to break our opponents down, we were 3-0 up and I had scored all three with varying degrees of both intended and unintended audacity!

Two more Inland Revenue goals compounded DTI's misery, and there was still enough time for me to latch on to a mistimed clearance and thrash a low drive past the goalie's right hand to wrap up a stunning 6-0 victory. I was therefore eagerly looking forward to playing in my first Lewis Cup Final and hoped to add to the nine goals I had already scored in that year's competition, but my hopes were about to be cruelly dashed by torn ankle ligaments, suffered whilst playing for my Saturday side at the time, Ely City.

I arrived on the day of the Lewis Cup Final against DHSS Newcastle, hoping and praying that the intensive treatment I had received since the injury would enable me to play some part in the tie. The fitness test with trainer Nick Parry however, quickly dispelled those hopes. I could move freely, but as soon as I kicked the ball with my right foot I was in intense pain. So it was with tears welling in my eyes that I ruefully informed manager John Heapy I wouldn't be able to make it. I did consider pretending that I was fit enough purely to be in the starting line-up, but that would have been unfair to my team-mates, my manager and myself.

I therefore viewed from the stands as John Wilson – and Pete Tilley, who moved up from midfield to accompany him in attack – tore DHSS Newcastle apart to win the Lewis Cup. The final score was 6-4, but it was about as one-sided a 6-4 match as you are ever likely to witness; DHSS Newcastle scored in seconds after Billy McLaren's defensive blunder, but other than that were simply never in it. As I watched this very open encounter unfold, I had to wonder how many goals a fit Steve Green might have contributed.

Next on the agenda for a clearly unfit 'Midge' Green was the aforementioned 1982/1983 Sunday League Cup Final against Newmarket Valley. Again I was hoping and praying that my right ankle would be strong enough to participate, but equally I knew that a fitness test was pointless because Crusaders needed me to be on the pitch, no matter what. For the Inland Revenue Football Club I may have been a valued component, but for Ely Crusaders I was an indispensable talisman. As someone in the crowd apparently commented that day, "Steve Green is the player who makes Crusaders tick."

I therefore ran out on to the Histon FC pitch with my loyal team-mates, and with the ball at my feet during the warm-up I attempted to kick it into the goal from six yards. Once again intense pain was the reward for my efforts, so I knew the prognosis; I had no option but to play the tie without kicking the ball with my natural foot.

The final began well, with Gary Chilvers producing a skidding free-kick that made the most of the damp conditions to put us in front early on. Newmarket equalised soon afterwards, but our lead was restored in the 20th minute. I collected the ball midway inside the opposition half, and would normally have curled a right-foot pass out wide to full-back Richard Goodjohn, who was a brilliant crosser and the supplier of countless opportunities for me from wide positions. But because I was unable to use my right foot at all, I was forced to improvise, and instead of protecting the ball as normal, I had to allow it to go underneath my right foot and virtually into the possession of my marker. Just before it reached him however, I used my left foot to squirt the ball into Goodjohn's path on the right and then made my way towards the Newmarket penalty area. His subsequent cross was – as usual – unerring, and in the centre of the penalty area, 15 yards from goal, I rose above the Valley defence and powered a header over the hands of goalkeeper Tony

Coombs and into the roof of the net to make it 2-1 – my 20th Sunday goal of that campaign.

We were good value for our half-time lead, and had I stayed on I am convinced we would have won (naturally!), but in the 65th minute Valley midfielder Martin Marris tackled me from behind and my final effort was over. Having played over an hour without once kicking the ball with my natural foot, I was carried off and spent the rest of the match laying in the dressing room with an ice pack on my ankle. I hoped we could hold on, but was brought news of Valley's equaliser – a disputed penalty – and I feared the worst in extra-time. Another disputed penalty put us behind for the first time and we were 4-2 down by the time central defender Stuart Norman nodded home with seconds of extra-time remaining, making the final score 4-3. It had been a bone-crunching encounter littered with bookings, and was also the last chapter in a decade-long rivalry between the two clubs.

CHAPTER THREE: 'Chic' Cooper

Ely Crusaders under-18 manager Eric 'Chic' Cooper was the man who changed everything for me. By the time I was playing (on occasion) for Brian Atkin at under-16 level, 'Chic' had already noticed me and eventually voiced his opinion that I was being 'under-used'. In the opening 11 league and cup fixtures in 1974/1975, the preferred strike force was Marcus Humphry alongside Adrian 'Bunter' Thompson. I had no problem as far as Marcus was concerned, because he was fast, good in the air and an accomplished finisher. Adrian on the other hand, had not (in my opinion) progressed much at all since first appearing in a Crusaders shirt.

So with a league game at Comberton on the horizon, Marcus was of course an automatic selection with 14 league and cup goals to his credit, and 'Bunter' had scored seven. At that stage of the season, I had managed only three, and one of those had been in our only league defeat to date at Teversham. I was in the starting line-up at Comberton however, and made the most of it by helping myself to a hat-trick even though we eventually suffered a 5-4 defeat.

It was at this point in time (as far as I know) that 'Chic' made it clear to Brian that I was almost certainly the best forward he had available to him. Marcus – with whom I would subsequently establish a productive striking partnership at Ely Crusaders – finally notched 30 league and cup goals that season, but I bagged 15 in the last 11 matches of the campaign and was now established in the team ahead of 'Bunter'. Neither Marcus nor Adrian would ever come close to outscoring me again – at least not in a Crusaders shirt.

Part-way through the following 1975/1976 season I had scored 23 goals in 15 league and cup appearances, and the last of those goals was a header in the 10-1 home win against Cambridge-based Manorians, completing my hat-trick. What apparently impressed 'Chic' was not necessarily the number of goals I was scoring, but the manner in which I was scoring them. The third against Manorians came from a right wing cross which reached me about six yards from goal. I could have nodded it anywhere and probably still have scored, but I guided it gently – almost back in the direction from which the ball came – just inside the far post. In fact, about as far from any opposition player as it could possibly have been.

I went on to score 11 more goals in eight remaining games for the under-16s, which meant I had been on the scoresheet in 10 successive appearances – including one in which I even began the game as our goalkeeper at Coton! By that time however, 'Chic' had already selected me for the second half of his under-18s campaign, and at last there was someone who believed in my abilities. I suddenly found myself playing twice on a Sunday; in the mornings for 'Chic' with the under-18s, and in the afternoons for Brian with the under-16s!

Ely Crusaders under-16s eventually finished fourth in the league behind Newmarket Valley, Cambridge Hornets and Cambridge Crusaders. Valley beat us 5-1 and 5-0 in the league, but won the title only because of our controversial win over Hornets, who had already beaten us 4-2 in the league and 3-2 in the last eight of the League Cup. We were leading Hornets 2-1 at home when their midfielder Guy Loveday broke through our defence and stroked the ball home for the equaliser. His well-placed shot went through the back of the net however, and the referee did not know if it was a goal. It was fairly obvious to everyone else that the ball went in, but the referee finally awarded a goal-kick and we went straight up the other end and scored to make the game safe!

We finally got the better of Valley that season by coming from behind to win the semi-final of the Knock-out Cup 4-3, but Hornets then got their revenge on us by winning the final 2-0 on my 16th birthday. I have a 'Star Wars' birthday by the way; May the fourth be with you....

As a final footnote to the 1975/1976 under-16 campaign, I recall a friendly match at Weston Colville School against a Huddersfield side called Birkby. I had scored within minutes, and then struck again as we ran them ragged. In fact, I was having such an influence on the game that Brian substituted me after 35 minutes to save our visitors from even greater embarrassment! It eventually ended 7-1, but my confidence was undoubtedly growing at this stage by virtue of my involvement with the under-18 team, albeit as a 15-year old.

Ely Crusaders under-18s were eventually destined for some success of their own, having experienced a disappointing end to their league campaign behind the likes of Cambridge Hornets and Cambridge United Youths. My only regret at this stage was missing out on the under-18s FA Youth Cup encounter with Norwich City Youths, which ended in a goalless draw. Crusaders apparently deserved to win the tie and indeed had chances to do so, but they just missed that cutting edge which I might have provided. ('Chic' mentioned afterwards that in hindsight he wished he had selected me. Norwich made no mistake in the replay at Carrow Road however, winning it 6-0).

My first experience of under-18 football – against good quality opposition too – was in the Cambridgeshire Sunday Youth League Cup competition. This – due to the comparatively small number of teams that had participated in the league – was simply a repeat of the campaign that had already taken place in the first half of the season, thus providing more fixtures for all the teams than would have been the case with a pure knock-out competition.

In the first of our eight fixtures in the 'league-based' League Cup, a late strike from Andy Peacock secured a 1-0 home victory against the favourites Cambridge United Youths. Cambridge-based St Andrews were the next visitors to Downham Road, and I scored my first goals for the under-18s, grabbing a hat-trick in our 6-0 romp. Defender Geoff Seymour then struck both goals in a 2-1 success at Cambridge United, and I was on target again as we thrashed St Andrews 5-0 away from home.

Cambridge Hornets were the next visitors to Downham Road, and things didn't look too promising as we trailed 2-0 at the interval. Peacock pulled one back after the break however, and I salvaged a 2-2 draw with a back header that only just crept over the line.

After a 4-3 friendly win against Dutch side Aeolus of Rotterdam, and a 3-1 Youth League Cup triumph at Mildenhall in which I netted once, we were drawn to play Cambridge United Youths again in the semi-finals of the Cambridgeshire County Youth Cup. Still smarting from two recent odd-goal defeats by us, United perhaps thought that we might be intimidated by playing the tie at the Abbey Stadium itself. For a while it looked as if this tactic might work, because we conceded a goal in the opening half and still trailed well into the second period. But the 'U's had reckoned without our secret weapon – Alan 'The Assassin' Alsop.

Alan was a year or so older than me, but lived about 80 yards from my house and we were very good friends. We often played football together at the local parks, but seldom represented the same team competitively. He was one of those players who had a wonderful touch (although he never kicked a ball with his right foot, or headed it for that matter), but he never really produced the talent on the pitch that he undoubtedly possessed. On this particular day however, he certainly did.

Alan strolled on to the Abbey pitch and – in an unfamiliar striking role – soon rifled home the equaliser; with his left foot, of course. So we were in extra-time. Bear in mind that before this day, I had never seen Alan score a single competitive goal (and believe me, he didn't score many!) Suddenly, Crusaders were the dominant force against their illustrious opponents, and Alan struck again. 'Paddy' Collins added a third, and I compounded United's misery by firing home from close range to make the final score 4-1. But this was Mr Alsop's day, and against the odds we were through to the final of the competition.

The next match was effectively the Youth League Cup decider away at Cambridge Hornets, and it turned out to be a game that changed my life in so many ways.

With seven goals in as many under-18 cup appearances, I was feeling pretty pleased with myself. I was however, in for a very rude awakening. Hornets were in no mood to accommodate a young upstart like me, and in a goalless first half I had about as much impact as a lemonade stand at the Cambridge Beer Festival.

At half-time, 'Chic' took me to one side, and explained to me in no uncertain terms that if I did not get 'stuck in', I would remain peripheral to the action. Now in his own playing days, 'Chic' was renowned as an uncompromising hard man. He was built like me, headed the ball like me, and scored goals like me. Only he was as hard as granite. That toughness – despite my appearance* – was clearly absent from my game at that point in time, and I needed to acquire it fast. In about five minutes to be precise.

When I was eight years old, I lost my two front teeth in a playground accident during a game of 'British

Bulldog'. I therefore wore a plate which I removed before each game, and my toothless appearance was probably enough to put the frighteners on most players my age. Players in their late teens and adult players however, were not quite so easily intimidated by my ugliness.

Maybe I took the manager's criticism too personally, or his advice too literally, but in the second half against mighty Cambridge Hornets I was a different animal to the one they had intimidated in the first. I didn't score, but Hornets suddenly and painfully became aware of my presence as I rampaged around the pitch like a bear looking for the woods.

My team-mates appeared to profit from this ursine transformation, and goals from substitute Alsop (the last one I ever saw him score), 'Paddy' Collins and the genial Alan Moore secured a remarkable 3-0 victory against Vince Donnelly's much-vaunted Hornets.

I struck my final two goals of the campaign as we wrapped up the Youth League Cup with a 4-1 home win against Mildenhall, and although we subsequently lost the County League Cup Final 2-0 against Wisbech in extra-time I had my first ever trip abroad where we were hosted in s'Hertogenbosch by Dutch amateur side Beatrix '63. We finished second in an under-18 multi-national tournament (losing 2-1 in the final to our hosts after I had levelled the scores), but gained our revenge in the 90-minute friendly clash when we finally solved the offside 'riddle' posed by their defence.

In those days you were offside if you were behind the opposition defence (bar two defenders, one of which usually but not always included the goalkeeper) when the ball was played forward, no matter what you happened to be doing. You could be picking your nose on the touchline, whilst the ball was being passed 70 yards away to the other side, but you would still be caught out by the linesman's flag. So the Beatrix defence pushed up relentlessly and caught us offside time and time again. At half-time 'Chic' instructed us (the forwards) to sprint back with the defenders, and our midfielders ('Paddy' Collins in particular) could then sprint through from their own half on to any through ball hit into the open space. It worked a treat. Collins scored to make it 2-2, and an own goal from a Beatrix defender being pressurised by Collins then handed us the victory.

By this stage of my career – as a 15-year-old – I had started to make my mark in adult football on Saturdays, and – somehow – I also found time on Sundays to play some men's football with Ely Park Rangers. For them I scored four league goals in as many games (fellow striker Dave Rudnicki, one of the best finishers I ever saw, scored a mere 11 in five games!), but my Saturday experiences at this time were perhaps more noteworthy.

Rudnicki was the prolific centre-forward for Division 1B County League side Stretham Hotspurs, so after one of our Sunday matches together for Ely Park Rangers I expressed an interest in playing Saturday football (as if playing for three Sunday teams was not sufficient!) Dave said that Stretham Reserves were in action at Little Downham Swifts Reserves in six days' time, so the best thing I could do was to simply turn up and tell the manager that I wanted a game!

So that's what I did. I put my football boots in a plastic carrier bag, slung the bag in the basket on the front of my bike and cycled the three or so miles to the playing field in Little Downham. You were allowed just one substitute per team in those days, but Stretham only had 11 players so I sat on the sidelines and – as an unregistered player – awaited my big chance.

Manager Les Thistlethwaite (try saying that after a crate of Pinot Grigio) brought this opportunistic 15-year old on with 20 minutes remaining, but the writing was already on the wall by that stage and we eventually lost by the narrow margin of 9-4!

I was substitute again the following week (now a bona fide Stretham Hotspurs recruit) at Lode Reserves, but this time was introduced with five minutes of the first half remaining. I scored my first Stretham goal with a bicycle kick at the far post, but we went down 6-3. I had however, made my mark, and after watching from the sidelines throughout a 7-2 win at CDP Pye, made my full debut at home to Fordham's 'A' team. As you may have already gathered, there were plenty of goals in County League Division 4B, and this match was no exception. We ran riot that day, with Steve Jackson hitting five and me contributing a hat-trick as Fordham's third team were humbled 13-3!

The following week saw a brutal match at West Wratting abandoned after 76 minutes because of bad light. This was because one of the home players broke a leg, with a crack that sounded like lightning felling a tree. There was a lengthy delay waiting for the ambulance to arrive (it took nearly as long to get there as it had taken the players to walk from the remote changing 'facilities' to the West Wratting pitch!), and having led 2-0 by virtue of Jimmy Turner's double, it was all square by the time of the abandonment.

My progress within the ranks of Stretham Hotspurs Reserves was such that when the Ely Standard report was published after the following week's 1-0 defeat to eventual Lower Junior Cup winners Benwick Athletic, it mentioned that the team sorely missed the "unavailable 15-year-old Steve Green".

Our next match was at Division 4B leaders Longstanton, but our unbeaten run continued as I contributed a hat-trick to Stretham's 5-3 win. We defeated the same opponents 2-1 at home the following week, and then faced local rivals Sutton United Reserves in an attempt to continue our rise up the table. It should be borne in mind that this game occurred before I underwent my transformation from a boy to a man in the under-18 clash with Cambridge Hornets, and I duly received my first 'proper' physical introduction to the world of adult football. Perhaps as a result of my burgeoning local reputation, I was kicked, punched, elbowed and thumped in the stomach as the 'old heads' in the Sutton team showed me (and put me on) the ropes, but we still managed a narrow victory.

Until the aforementioned Hornets 'education' came about, my confidence was undoubtedly undermined for a while as we (Stretham Reserves) lost four on the bounce before I made my first team debut in a 3-0 home win against Camden, with Mr Rudnicki naturally scoring twice. One of the things I didn't like about playing for Stretham's first team however, was that they had the proverbial 'cheat' as a linesman. I suppose it might have been because he didn't know any better, but he seemed to act on the basis that the ball being knocked into Stretham's half was sufficient reason to raise his flag. I even saw him flag a striker offside in a one-on-one situation when the striker knocked the ball past a covering defender and ran round him to 'score' (it was disallowed, naturally!) I have never condoned cheating.

In the 1975/1976 season – including school matches – I made a total of 78 competitive appearances, scoring 72 times. In the following season I managed to exceed that number of competitive appearances, but goals – for reasons that will become evident – were somewhat harder to come by.

CHAPTER FOUR: Cambridge City

At the start of the 1976/1977 season, aged 16, I joined Cambridge City with a view to playing for their under-18 team in the Chiltern Youth League. In my opinion the standard was quite high, and each team (usefully in my view) was allowed to field one player who was not a youth player.

Our first competitive fixture was at home to local rivals Cambridge United, who scored four second half goals to hand us a 5-1 mauling. Nigel Dixon – a diminutive, cocky, but talented midfielder scored our only goal that evening, but – perhaps like me it could be argued – his eventual status in the game never matched his obvious ability.

It was perhaps fortunate that I was joined in City's youth ranks at various points in time by the likes of Mick Hennebry, his brother Pat, Gary Chilvers and Ian Smith, who were all team-mates from my Sunday side Ely Crusaders, so I didn't feel friendless at my new club.

Youngsters would probably find it hard to believe nowadays, but I often had to hitch a lift to and from Cambridge twice a week for training, let alone for matches. Youth Team manager Eric Simper who also lived in Ely, sometimes provided us with a lift to the Milton Road ground, but work commitments prevented this from happening all the time so schoolboys like myself had to travel the 16 or so miles in the best way we could. Cambridge railway station was inconveniently situated on the other side of town, so getting lifts with potential axe-murderers was the only viable option for us lads who came from outside Cambridge.

In our opening Chiltern League match of the campaign I scored a spectacular second half equaliser to open my account in the 2-2 home clash with Harlow Town, and in midweek – under floodlights for the first time in my football career – I was amongst the goal scorers in a 4-2 FA Youth Cup First Qualifying Round tie at Wellingborough.

I was then on target again as we recovered from being a goal down at the interval to beat Hitchin Town 4-1 at home in the league, before a run of three successive away defeats at Luton Town, Hoddesdon and Vauxhall Motors produced no goals for me or anyone else in the team. I particularly remember the 3-0 defeat we suffered at Luton-based Vauxhall, but only for the fact that their pitch was perhaps the best playing surface I ever encountered.

After three successive defeats and more than 270 minutes without a goal, I started to receive a degree of criticism from certain quarters; in particular from team-mate Nigel Dixon. Our next match was in the Second Qualifying Round of the FA Youth Cup at home to a Hitchin Town side we had already beaten, so I was hopeful of progressing further in the competition. I hooked the ball home to open the scoring, but the visitors grabbed two before half-time and added a third after the break.

We looked down and out, but when the goalkeeper received a back-pass at his feet (which in those days he was allowed to pick up) I had a moment of inspiration. Having followed the back-pass in, I would normally have wheeled away because the goalkeeper had the ball absolutely in his control. But I kept going straight towards him, and before he had time to do anything about it I had crunched the ball between his legs and followed up behind him to tap the ball over the line. (Several years later – again before the change to the back-pass rule – I did the very same thing for Ely City to score the first goal in a 2-0 win at Brantham Athletic, just before the Town & Country League Cup Final against Lowestoft Town took place).

Time was still running out on us in the aforementioned FA Youth Cup tie, but with seconds remaining full-back Mark Watson laid the ball up to me on the edge of the 'D'. Controlling the ball on my chest and turning in the same movement, I fired a swerving drive into the top right-hand corner of the net to earn a 3-3 draw and a replay.

It was one of those rare occasions when opposition defenders would turn and congratulate you on doing something remarkable. The other time I recall that happening was during a tour match with Littleport Town against the Dutch hosts Beatrix '63's 2nd XI. With my back to goal and fully 30 yards out, I feinted one way and then the other before spinning and unleashing a diagonal left-foot drive into the right top corner of the net. Instead of bemoaning the concession of a goal, several of the Beatrix defenders simply turned to me and applauded!

It is perhaps worth mentioning again at this stage, that I am naturally a right-footed player. Crusaders manager 'Chic' Cooper however, instilled in me the need to become proficient with both feet, so – as with my heading – I practiced for hours with my 'wrong' foot. In fact, as hard as one might find this to believe, my left foot became technically more proficient than my 'natural' foot. As a result, defenders never knew on which side I would take them on. It didn't matter to me either, because I could do it equally well on either flank.

That's one thing that never ceases to amaze me about modern footballers. Some are paid hundreds of thousands of pounds a week, yet you hear commentators say "Oh, he would have preferred that on his stronger foot," or "That's a tame effort, but it was on his weaker side." What? These are so-called professionals! Why don't they practice?

After my FA Youth Cup hat-trick against Hitchin, I went through something of a goal drought with Cambridge City

Youths, even though I was perhaps still developing other aspects of my game. We crashed out of the FA Youth Cup 5-3 at Hitchin in the replay, and I added only two goals to my tally in the next 10 outings – one of which was a header in our 3-1 home Chiltern League victory against Letchworth which cost me a painful 'egg' on the left temple!

Our next match was at Cambridge United under the Abbey Stadium lights, and that was certainly a night to remember – for all the wrong reasons. United fielded several players who had already experienced Football League action, and on this occasion we were pulverised by the likes of winger Jamie Murray and midfielder Floyd Streete.

We were eventually humbled 8-0, and I particularly recall one of the goals from Streete, a 40-yard 'howitzer' which went precisely where he intended it – straight into the top left-hand corner and beyond the reach of goalkeeper Kevin Murray, who was certainly good enough to expect not to have been beaten from that range. It didn't have the purity of the strike from Ian Smith (more of that later) which was the best shot I ever saw, but it certainly had all of the power.

At this point in time, it became apparent that I had some way to go before even considering a professional career in football, but despite my recent lack of goals I was starting to get noticed by Cambridge City's first team management. I did not play in the City Youth Team's next two matches against Sunday side Manorians in the First Round of the Munns Cup, because I had already committed myself to Ely Crusaders in that competition. City were held to a 2-2 draw by Manorians in the opening clash, but progressed 2-0 in the replay.

I already had reason to believe that the under-18 Ely Crusaders Sunday team was superior to Cambridge City's equivalent line-up, because I played for both and during the 1976/1977 season we (Crusaders) had defeated Manorians 10-0, 5-0 and 5-1. This was not the reason I preferred Crusaders to City when it came to the Munns Cup however; it was a question of loyalty. Loyalty to the Crusaders players I had grown up with, but in particular the man – 'Chic' Cooper – who was responsible for moulding me into the player I had now become.

Perhaps 'Chic' and my Crusaders team-mates understood my attributes better than Eric Simper and my Cambridge City Youth team-mates, although I think the Cambridge boys at least got an inkling when – towards the end of the season – we had a friendly arranged against the Cambridgeshire Colts League representative side at under-15 level.

The Colts representative side turned up a player short, so I agreed to play for them instead of City to even up the numbers. I performed in a relatively unfamiliar midfield role, but helped to humble the City boys as my young team-mates and I ran out 6-4 winners. The embarrassment of the result was not lost on the City management team either, but even in my absence they were held 3-3 in the re-match a few weeks later.

In fairness, I had by that time already got some first team experience under my belt. I was taken along as substitute for the Southern League North match at Gloucester City, and with the team holding a 3-0 lead at the start of the second half manager Dave Worthington – brother of ex-England international Frank Worthington – promised me that I would be introduced to the action. Gloucester managed to pull a couple back however, so the 'boss' (as he liked to be called) decided that this was not the time to give a debut to the 16-year old striker sitting alongside him.

Tony Rule – who was my PE Teacher at St Mary's School in Ely – scored late on to secure a 4-2 win, but I felt a bit disappointed because I was hoping to make my first senior appearance as a 16-year old. This duly happened in the subsequent visit to Corby Town however, owing to an injury to key striker Alan Doyle.

Doyle – who had been with Chelsea in the early part of his career – was built like me and had razor-sharp instincts in front of goal. His involvement in play outside the box was fairly limited by comparison, but no-one cared much because he contributed more than 40 goals that season. If I was to make a breakthrough into the first team, I had to accept that it was very unlikely to be at his expense.

I played the whole match at Corby alongside Steve Mahoney, and although I thought I did OK I failed to convert a couple of half-chances that came my way and we lost 1-0.

I was quickly in first team action again during the midweek East Anglian Cup tie with Harwich & Parkeston, and although we recovered a two-goal interval deficit thanks to a Mahoney double, it finished 3-3 after extra-time. In the next league match at home to Cheltenham Town I played up front with Doyle for the first time, and he scored the only goal of the game, albeit after I had been substituted on the hour mark. I was then back on the substitute bench for the extraordinarily long trip to Oswestry Town, and was gutted not to at least get a run-out even though we came from behind to win 3-1.

I was back with the Youth Team for a few games after this, and when I next found myself in the first team starting line-up it was in an unfamiliar midfield role for the visit of Enderby Town. It was a real battle, and they had a very experienced, balding playmaker called Neil Mathens. The two of us went in for a challenge midway through the second half and I accidentally went over the top of the ball. The referee clearly appreciated that there was no intent because he didn't even book me, but Mathens' team-mates viewed matters differently and extracted their own retribution. I stood up to the physical assault however, and duly apologised to Mathens when the final whistle signalled the last action in a 2-2 draw.

My last first team football of the campaign was in the East Anglian Cup Qualifying Round replay at Harwich, where I crossed for Mahoney to score, but we were beaten 2-1. From then on whenever I was substitute, I was not used. I started to feel like substitute goalkeepers do nowadays; the only way I would get involved was if somebody got injured.

My failure to make a decisive break into the first team ranks at Cambridge City was disappointing, even though I had only just turned 17 years of age. My home senior club Ely City was apparently monitoring the situation, and because they played in a different (lower) league I was – with Cambridge City's permission – signed up to play in a couple of Eastern Counties League matches towards the end of the season.

The first was at home to Gorleston, who were always a powerful force at that level in the 1970s and 1980s. My strike partner on the day was Derek Waters, the type of player who would demolish your house with a wrecking ball rather than knock on the door to see if anyone was home, and who probably thought that 'finesse' was the French word for 'fairy'.

In those days the goalposts at Ely City's Paradise ground were square (nowadays they are always round), and Waters bludgeoned a shot towards the inside of the right-hand post. The Laws of Physics dictate that the ball should have hit the corner of the post and rebounded out at an unpredictable angle, but Derek's shot made a strange sound like someone slapping a pig with cricket bat and the ball inexplicably crashed into the net. I remain convinced to this day that the shot took a crescent-shaped chunk out of the post!

In the second period (and remember these were the days when back passes could be picked up by the goalkeeper), Gorleston defender Chris Watts (later to become a team-mate of mine at Kings Lynn) slid a back-pass diagonally towards his penalty spot from the right-back position. What he didn't realise was that his goalkeeper was only a few yards behind him at the corner of the penalty area. My first goal in semi-professional football could not have been simpler. Even so, I did touch the ball forward a couple of yards before side-footing home, as the goalkeeper was making rapid strides in his attempt to recover Watts' blunder. Too late. Two-nil.

My next Ely City appearance was in midweek at Thetford Town, and the goal I scored there was rather odd too. A cross came into the six-yard box and I was there, right on top of the goalkeeper. He managed to catch the ball, but as he brought it down he did so right on my forehead. I did not actually move to 'head' the ball, but the force of the 'keeper bringing it down directly on to my bonce was sufficient to release it from his grasp and the ball flew high into the net. Having trailed at the midway point, we eventually ran out 3-1 winners.

In between playing for Cambridge City, Cambridge City Youths, Ely City, Ely Crusaders Youths, City of Ely College First XI, the County Youth team and the Colts League under-15 representative side (!), I also managed to fit in nine appearances for Ely Crusaders' senior team and 10 appearances for Stretham Hotspurs' first team!

I scored in the Creake Shield Final as Stretham were

beaten 4-2 by Foxton, and I was also on target for Ely Crusaders senior team in the 4-3 Soham Charity Cup Final win against Soham Town's Sunday team. We had reached the final at the expense of Stretham (of all teams!), turning a 3-0 interval deficit into a 7-3 success at windswept Qua Fen Common.

I was quite pleased with my goal in the final against Soham, having allowed a right wing pass to go across the front of my body before directing a shot inside the near post with the outside of my left foot. Soham defender Micky Robinson, who was later to become my manager and good friend at Soham Town Rangers on Saturdays, turned to me immediately afterwards exclaiming "You lucky bastard!" He knew very well that I had been anything but lucky. A bastard maybe.

So after playing 78 competitive matches in 1975/1976, I somehow managed to better that with 82 appearances in 1976/1977, plus five as unused substitute. It was one of the last of those 82 appearances that arguably had the most significant impact on my footballing life.

CHAPTER FIVE: Club v Country Bumpkins

Having won 3-1 at Wisbech Town Youths in a very tough First Round encounter in the 1976/1977 Munns Cup, Ely Crusaders Youths were drawn away to – yes, you've guessed it – Cambridge City Youths.

I was well up for it. Ely Crusaders was not a popular team as far as the Cambridge lads were concerned, and Nigel Dixon in particular had an unjustified superiority complex in my opinion. So much so that when he was playing for Manorians against us in a Sunday League match, he had the temerity to criticise me for thumping a 20-yard shot against the bar, even though I was already well on my way to a five-goal haul during his side's 10-0 humiliation.

In the Munns Cup tie at Milton Road I put Crusaders 1-0 up with an opportunistic strike, but Nigel scored for City as the first half finished 2-2. As the second period got underway however, we took complete control of the match. We were leading 3-2 when City centre-half Kevin Herridge attempted to find goalkeeper Kevin Murray with a short back-pass. I nipped in to intercept the ball and nudged it to the right – out of Murray's reach – before firing high into the net from the narrowest of angles.

I then won (and badly screwed wide) a penalty kick which could have completed my hat-trick, and City pulled back a late goal which provided them with a shred of respectability. The scoreline of 4-3 however, in no way reflected the superiority Crusaders had on the day.

We went on to lose the Munns Cup Final 5-2 against Cambridge United Youths, but when you consider that they had already beaten their City rivals 5-1, 3-1 and 8-0, the result didn't look quite so bad for the 'country bumpkins' from Ely.

In 1977/1978 we inevitably drew Cambridge City again in the same competition, and as the tie approached I was called into the manager's office by Dave Worthington. He referred to the cup tie in question and said in no uncertain terms that this time I would be playing for Cambridge City Youths. I simply replied "No, I won't." He re-iterated that I would, adding that if I didn't, then I could leave the club. I responded by saying "OK."

The ridiculous thing is that the tie never took place because Cambridge City Youths were 'unable to raise a team'. The truth I believe, is that the club was so embarrassed by their Youth Team having been outplayed by a 'bumpkin' Sunday outfit a year earlier, that they didn't wish to risk suffering the same indignity again. So with that, my career at Cambridge City drew prematurely to a close.

Rightly or wrongly, I made my decision for reasons of pure loyalty. Crusaders manager 'Chic' Cooper had taught me lots of things, and had shaped me into the player I had become. The only thing Worthington ever taught me was that – when eating chicken in a restaurant – it was acceptable to pick a piece up with your hand in order to eat it, so long as you only used one hand! (Fortunately when it came to things like clapping and tying shoe laces, I already knew that you ideally needed to use two hands). I would like to place on record my sincere thanks to Mr Worthington for sharing that particular piece of culinary wisdom with me at such a (food) critical stage of my football career.

'Chic' though, taught me plenty, including the basic principles of playing in goal! Why? Well, he reasoned that as a striker, if you fully understood the problems a goalkeeper had, then you were better equipped to take advantage of those problems.

'Chic' – who as you may already have guessed, had FA coaching qualifications to his name – seldom raised his voice before, during or after games in which he was involved. Instead he took notes during the game, and explained things in a way no other coach or manager ever did either before this period, during it or since. For example, he emphasised the importance of retaining possession. He elaborated on this by pointing out that – with 22 players on the pitch – you would – if you were lucky – have possession of the ball for three or four minutes each match. So why would you want to give it away? Common sense of course, but so many players needlessly concede possession by attempting passes or through balls that are simply not on. You don't need to play forward all the time, and the modern professional game very much reflects that.

He emphasised the need for immaculate ball control. If you immediately had the ball under your spell, you had so much more time to do with it what you wanted.

He highlighted the importance of movement. Too many players think only about the ball, and not what impact they can have in terms of creating time and space for others. I may have hated training, but as you can possibly tell by the fact that I was playing around 80 games per season, I was supremely fit. As a striker, this made me difficult to mark. One minute I was on the left wing, the next in midfield, the next clearing a corner from defence, and the next heading a ball on the edge of the opposition penalty area.

I recall once when I was playing for Ely City at home to Clacton Town, that one of the exhausted opposition defenders rested his hand on my shoulder in the second half, and asked me a simple question: "When are you going to stop running?"

The ironic thing was that (in hindsight) opposing players perhaps appreciated my attributes rather more than some of my team-mates. If as a striker, I didn't score for Cambridge City, I was deemed a failure. Maybe though, I was a better all-round player than they realised.

I believe that I did have the ability to play at a higher level, and possibly even as a professional. Worse players than me have played in the Football League, and better players than me have likewise failed to make it.

So in 15 appearances for the Cambridge City first team, most of which were not for the full 90 minutes (I was also unused substitute on 10 occasions), I had just a single goal to show for my efforts. But what a goal it was!

I was making my seasonal bow in the 1977/1978 East Anglian Cup First Qualifying Round at home to Cheshunt, and after Steve Kearns had put us in front we were building another attack down the right. When the cross came in, the goalkeeper was stretching but managed to fist the ball out 20 yards to where I had advanced. If I had taken the time to control the ball, the 'keeper might have had time to reposition himself and defenders could have closed me down, so I launched myself for a diving header instead. I could not have connected with the ball more sweetly, and the goalkeeper's hand was still on its way down from delivering the punch when the header flew back past it into the top left-hand corner of the net.

City captain and subsequent Ely City colleague Martin Murray (elder brother of goalkeeper Kevin Murray) once described me as the best header of a ball (for my size) that he had seen, and certainly that power in the air became an integral part of my game. As 'Chic' once told me, being good in the air is nothing to do with being tall; it is everything to do with timing. When – much later in my footballing life – I played back in defence, I was pretty much indomitable in the air. As a striker however, I thrived on crosses, but you need a chain of supply and of course not every team has one.

Crosses were another integral part of his thinking. 'Chic' reckoned that 80% of goals were scored from crosses of one type or another, and the further down the field those crosses could be delivered – so that defenders were forced to face their own goal – the better. So whenever I received the ball in wide positions, I was acutely aware of the need to cross accurately, and fortunately I could do so with either foot.

Centre-forwards I played alongside for the Great Britain & Northern Ireland Inland Revenue team included European Golden Boot winner Dave Taylor, and England semi-professional Paul Patey. Both led the front line as target men, and I would like to think that they both considered me to be a more than adequate striking partner. Although I scored my fair share of Lewis Cup goals for the Inland Revenue Football Club (54 in 52 appearances), I was very often the provider of goals for both of those players (unfortunately for me it was seldom the other way round!)

Patey was powerful, lightning fast, very useful in the air and a bulldozing finisher. Taylor had immaculate control, was deceptively quick and was a great header of the ball; a little selfish at times, but in terms of being a pure goalscorer he was absolutely clinical. Patey would virtually break the net with the ball, whereas Taylor would be more likely to coolly pass it into the corner.

Taylor was playing in the Welsh League for Porthmadog when he emerged as Europe's top scorer with 43 goals in the 1993/1994 season. The Cyprus FA had protested a couple of years earlier that the Golden Boot award was biased towards certain European Leagues (who for example, played more games), so between 1991 and 1996 the sponsors L'Equipe issued no awards. Adidas continued to present an award however, and in 1994 it was Taylor who entered the record books as the outright winner of that accolade.

My overall goal tally in 1976/1977 was still a respectable 62, but 40 of those were scored for Ely Crusaders Youths and the Ely Crusaders Senior Team. So for whatever reason, I had not made the required impact at Southern League level with Cambridge City, or indeed in the Chiltern Youth League with the same club.

There were a number of questions I had to consider. Was it because with Cambridge City, I was being played infrequently, and when I did play it was invariably out of position? Was it because with Cambridge City Youths, despite a reasonable understanding with the taller Steve Kearns which earned us first team debuts at the respective ages of 16 and 17, our under-18 squad was just not good enough to provide enough striking ammunition against the likes of Cambridge United, Luton Town, Hoddesdon Town and Hertford Town? Or was it quite simply, that I was not good enough to make the grade? Or a combination of all those factors to some degree or another?

Certain players (and I have seen very, very few) look good in any line-up. Record Cambridge City goalscorer Gary Grogan (who never played league football either to my knowledge) was one of the only ones that springs to mind. One of the only 'ordinary' players I ever encountered who could score lots of goals in a poor side was Richard Palmer at Soham Town Rangers. He had an uncanny knack of peeling off the last defender's shoulder on to long, hopeful through balls, and he had sufficient pace and power to nearly always get an effort on target. Many of them found the net, and overall he was a tireless and selfless runner for the team.

Me? I think that in the right team, I could have made an impact. But in truth, I perhaps never had the individual level of skill that on its own could have elevated me above the thousands of other footballers who harboured similar ambitions. 'Making it' in the world of professional football is I believe, seldom down to the ability of the individual alone; it is usually dependent on circumstance, coincidence and most of all, luck. (Although nowadays it seems pretty much dependent on hailing from anywhere but the British Isles).

The spectacular goal against Cheshunt did nothing in terms of advancing my claims for a regular place in the Cambridge City first team. I was substituted in that game with 25 minutes remaining, owing to the fact that the visitors had restored parity in the second half. Tony Rule blasted home the late 3-2 winner, but I was (apparently) out of favour. So I returned to the Youth Team ranks, and with Kearns retaining his first team place I was left to plough a lone furrow in the under-18 City attack.

I powered home a header from Steve Webb's corner for the only goal of the game at home to Hertford, and we then lost by the same 1-0 scoreline at Harlow before Kearns and I were reunited for the 2-0 East Anglian Junior Cup quarter-final reverse at home to Norwich City Youths. A 0-0 draw with Vauxhall Motors followed, and then came a home clash with Stevenage in which I grabbed both goals in a 2-1 success.

My first in that game came when a pass was played diagonally into the penalty area and I controlled it in my stride, using the outside of my right foot. In the same movement I then planted my left foot before lashing the ball home with my right, giving the goalkeeper no chance to set himself. After the game our 'keeper Kevin Murray said to me that only I could have scored that goal. This was a tremendous compliment from a goalkeeper I greatly admired, and who went on to play many first team games for Cambridge City.

When we were not playing on the same side however, Kevin hated the sight of me because I always seemed to score against him! It didn't matter if he was playing for Newmarket Valley, Saffron Walden Town, Haverhill Rovers or indeed Cambridge City Youths, I nearly always managed to find the net when he was in opposition.

My second goal for Cambridge City Youths in the Stevenage win saw me skip over two challenges and then hurdle the goalkeeper with the ball at my feet to score into an empty net. The team had now managed just three goals in five outings, but I had been responsible for them all. This earned me a first team recall and – in the absence of Doyle – I reprised my partnership with Kearns. We caused our opponents Kings Lynn some difficulties, but Mahoney's first half goal was cancelled out so we had to settle for a 1-1 draw.

The following night's Cambridge Evening News reported the fact that neither Kearns nor I had found the net, and went on to say that this was something that Doyle "would probably have achieved in the swirling conditions." I was therefore back as unplayed substitute for the next two meetings with Barry Town and Bridgend, but it seemed that I had at least impressed Kings Lynn more than I had the City management (so much so that at the start of the 1978/1979 season, having effectively been kicked out by City after the Munns Cup fiasco, I became a 'Linnets' player).

My next first team action for Cambridge City however, was in the Cambridgeshire Invitation Cup tie at Ely City, so in a way I was 'returning home'. I felt that I performed quite well in our 2-1 victory, and this proved to be one of only two occasions in my life when my mum came to watch me play.

The Cambridge City Youth Team was now faring a little better in my absence, but I was having to content myself with fleeting substitute appearances for the first team. I really hated being the 12th man, as I had been for all those years with the Ely Crusaders youngsters.

Cambridge United Youths were the next midweek opponents for Cambridge City under-18s, and I had been reliably informed that the league club was monitoring my progress. I had already played in a trial match for United on the Abbey all-weather surface, and had scored twice – both headers – in a 6-0 win against Soham United Youths. In the Chiltern League derby encounter with Cambridge United I did myself justice, glancing home a header from Ian Smith's raking left wing cross and hitting the bar with a lob during a 2-1 defeat. I also tested United goalkeeper Richard Powis on other occasions during the match, but still United were not tempted to move in for me. United scout Paddy Sowden was apparently asked about any individual performances that caught his eye, and was reported to have said: "I thought the lad Green did well again." I then thought that it was maybe only a matter of time, but the telephone never rang and my chance with Cambridge United never came.

In fact it was with Colchester United that I came closest to achieving my aim of playing league football. Cambridge City Youths entertained their Colchester counterparts in a friendly, and I scored the opening goal in an impressive 3-0 victory. Another friendly was then arranged – probably by 'Chic' Cooper, almost entirely for my benefit – between Colchester United Youths and Ely Crusaders Youths. On this occasion I was even more influential, scoring all three Crusaders goals in yet another 3-0 win. Consequently I found myself embarking on a close-season trip with Colchester United Youths to Brean Sands near

Weston-super-Mare, where an annual six-a-side tournament between southern-based Football League clubs was taking place. I was the only amateur player in the Colchester squad; everyone else was on contract for United.

Itching to get into the action on the first day, I had to stand on the touchline alongside manager Bobby Roberts and his assistant Ray Harford, who later became manager of Blackburn Rovers before his sadly premature death. My chance eventually came in the match against Southampton, whose side included – amongst others – Steve Moran who was to become a prolific goalscorer in the top flight. I remember noticing Southampton's legendary centre-half Jim McGrath towering above all other spectators on the touchline. I thought my moment had come when I latched on to a through ball and was clear behind the Southampton defence. As the goalkeeper advanced I pulled the trigger – my trusted left foot – and knew precisely where the ball was destined to go; diagonally into the top right-hand corner.

Suddenly I was down. Southampton's last defender had raced back and fouled me from behind. In a full-scale match it would have resulted in a penalty, but in this tournament the offence – whilst 15 yards from goal – took place outside the goalkeeper's area. I was still prostrate on the floor when Russell Cotton's quick-thinking saw him instantly ground the loose ball and pass square across the face of the goal for Tony Evans to side-foot home. Both of those players experienced plenty of league action for Colchester, but the opportunity for an unknown youngster from the backwaters of Ely had effectively come and gone. We eventually lost that game 2-1 and in fact failed to win a single match in the entire tournament against some admittedly very strong teams. I recall seeing the lanky, black striker Justin Fashanu in action for Norwich City Youths, and suddenly felt out of my depth. I was in all probability the only player in the entire tournament who was not already signed on professional terms with a Football League club.

The week ended, and on the last evening some of the Colchester lads decided that they would leave the Pontins complex and buy some booze for a 'secret' party. I went to bed early, but that didn't prevent Russell Cotton from entering the bedroom at one point and throwing some drink over me. I remained in bed and was still there when Harford entered the chalet demanding to know what the hell was going on. He threw open the door of the bedroom where I was, and noticed me in bed. He then castigated the rest of the 'professional' lads, pointing out that an amateur player was showing them all how to behave. It still didn't earn me a contract though, so I may as well have got pissed up with the rest of them.

CHAPTER SIX: The Great Crusade

As in the 1973/1974 season when Ely Crusaders under-14s won the Colts League title, there were only four teams in with a realistic chance of securing the 1977/1978 Cambridge & District Sunday Youth League, and 'Chic' Cooper's under-18 Crusaders side was again the least fancied of the quartet involved.

Cambridge United's Sunday Youth team was never as powerful as their Chiltern League line-up, but it was still extremely strong and Peter Reeve's side were again favourites to win it. Newmarket Valley and Histon FC were likewise strong contenders for the title. Valley's squad included the likes of goalkeeper Kevin Murray, Tony Marshall, Kevin Herridge, the Stanbridge brothers Trevor and David, Steve Webb and Steve Kearns, all of whom were my team-mates at Cambridge City.

Histon FC were the dark horses perhaps, with manager Vince Donnelly – a big name in the Construction Industry – having switched his allegiance from Cambridge Hornets. In doing so, he took with him all the best Hornets players, including midfield maestro Guy Loveday, central defender Chris Hutton and the mercurial Phil Prior.

Our first league outing of the season was a tough trip to Newmarket, where the hosts established a 1-0 interval lead and were good value for it. I fired in a 20-yard left-foot shot on the turn past Murray on the hour-mark however, and 1-1 was the way it finished. I was absent for the later return match at Downham Road, and it was the only game I missed all season for Crusaders. My team-mates nevertheless did the business, winning 3-2.

The only league game in which I played and failed to score in 1977/1978 was the crucial 1-0 home victory over Histon FC. I scored five in the 8-1 home win against the now weakened Hornets, and the same number in our 6-0 home victory against Soham Town Youths.

Hapless Histon Imps ultimately finished bottom of the table without a point to their name, and I managed a hat-trick of hat-tricks (nine goals) in the 15-2 win at their place, and another four as we thrashed them 15-1 at home.

The most crucial home goal I scored in that campaign however, was undoubtedly the one against Cambridge United. We trailed 2-0 in the second half, but Pat Hennebry pulled one back with a spectacular diving header and I then salvaged a point – and our unbeaten record – by nudging the ball past United goalkeeper John Black from eight yards to make the final score 2-2.

I then grabbed a brace in the 4-0 stroll at Soham Town, but we so very nearly came unstuck in our away clash with Cambridge Hornets. Having beaten them 8-1 at home and 11-0 away in the League Cup (a match in which I contributed seven goals), there seemed little reason to consider that they would cause us any problems. Pat Hennebry put us in front, but we were not playing at all well and the hosts deservedly equalised. We really could not afford to drop any points at that stage with Cambridge United, Newmarket Valley and Histon FC all breathing down our necks, and we rather fortunately scraped a 2-1 win courtesy of my scrappy late effort. It had been a real scare for us, but Cambridge United were in for an even bigger shock when they faced the same opponents soon afterwards. Hornets held them to a remarkable 0-0 draw – the only points that Hornets gained from any team outside the bottom two – which meant that a draw in our penultimate game at Histon FC would be enough for us to clinch the title. Our last fixture was away to Cambridge United, so we didn't really want to go there needing a result of any description.

With two games remaining (and remember, it was only two points for a win in those days), we were top on 18 points. Histon FC were second on 16, Cambridge United were third with the same number of points but with a worse goal difference and so couldn't win it because of the draw with Hornets. Back in 1973/1974 we had won our penultimate game at Valley to clinch the league championship. Could we possibly do the same against mighty Histon FC?

The maths was simple. If we won or drew the match, we were champions. If we lost the match, Histon would go top on goal difference and we would be left needing at least a draw in our final outing at United, where anything less than a draw would hand the title to Histon on goal difference ahead of both ourselves and United. All of us would have been on 18 points, just in front of Newmarket Valley on 17. That's how tight it was.

In past years Pat Hennebry's brother Mick had been an integral part of the Crusaders set-up, and although he was still playing for Cambridge City Youths he had dropped out of Sunday Youth football. 'Chic' knew the strengths of Histon FC, and was of course acutely aware of the importance of this particular game. So Mick Hennebry was persuaded to pull on the claret and blue of Ely Crusaders for one final time. His inclusion proved to be a master stroke by the manager.

Nullifying the midfield menace posed by Guy Loveday, Mick also found the time to cause damage in the heart of the Histon defence. I crashed home his free-kick at the far post early on, and Mick himself was also on target in an exhilarating first half. We initially held a 2-0 advantage, but the hosts pulled one back. We then led 3-1, but they responded with another goal before the break. It was touch and go all the way.

Histon predictably came on strong in the second period, but we struck again much against the run of play. The home goalkeeper fluffed a goal-kick, and the ball flew straight to Pat Hennebry who failed to control it. I was nearby however, and from 20-yards swept a powerful first-time side-foot shot low into the far corner beyond the reach of the stranded goalkeeper and just inside the post. Histon almost immediately reduced the deficit to a single goal again, but we were not the type of team to concede four or more goals in a game so we felt that the Youth League title was ours. It transpired that we were right, and the game ended 4-3 to our breathless relief.

In our final outing at Cambridge United we were keen to both retain our unbeaten league record and avenge a 2-0 defeat in the final of the League Cup at the hands of United, but it turned out to be one of those days for us. Marcus Humphry nodded us into the lead and I converted a penalty to put us two up, but a mistake from our goalkeeper Andy Morley allowed the hosts back into the game. It was very unfortunate for Andy because he had been brilliant and faultless throughout the campaign, but United were buoyed and eventually came back to beat us 3-2, clinching the runners-up berth ahead of Newmarket and Histon.

We subsequently drew Histon in the semi-finals of the Munns Cup, and I duly got my first unpalatable taste of man-to-man marking. Histon manager Vince Donnelly clearly saw me as the major threat to his side's ambitions after our 4-3 league win, so he drafted in the diminutive Barry Kempton to follow me all round the pitch. Kempton went on to play for Cambridge City's first team, but whilst in my view he was no footballer he was quite capable of following defensive orders to seek and destroy.

And that's exactly what he did. He stuck to me like the proverbial limpet. I found it quite disconcerting to be involved in a game during which an opponent continually stared at me and followed my every movement with complete disregard to the whereabouts of the ball. If I ran to the corner flag, he would follow me like a faithful puppy. The ball could have been 100 yards away and I might have been looking for a four-leaf clover for all he knew, but it made absolutely no difference to him. If I had sat down behind the Histon goal I'm certain he would have sat there beside me! I did manage to elude him once to cross for Marcus to nod in a first half equaliser, but otherwise I found it difficult to get away from this pest for whom I didn't much care anyway, having played against him previously. I can't deny that he did his job well however, and my threat was pretty much nullified in this particular game as we went down 3-1.

We didn't fare any better in the East Anglian Youth Cup semi-final, going down 1-0 to Rectory Rovers by virtue of a controversial penalty awarded in the last minute of extra-time. Consequently we failed to win any of the cup competitions in 1977/1978, but the league title was the thing we coveted most and we had secured that with a game to spare against three teams who might have expected to finish ahead of us.

I have already touched upon the hat-trick I scored in the friendly at Colchester United Youths, but I also managed to score three goals for the Ely Crusaders first team as both they and I tasted Senior Division action for the first time. That gave me a grand total of 50 goals in Crusaders colours during 1977/1978, earning me the Player-of-the-Year accolade for the first time in my career. Despite my best efforts, it would be another 24 years before I was next honoured by my fellow club members as the most valuable player in the team.

In the 1977/1978 season, Ely Crusaders under-18s scored a total of 93 goals, and we had no less than 17 different goalscorers, plus one from an opposition player. Even goalkeeper Andy Morley got in on the act with a penalty kick against Histon Imps! Of those 93 goals, I contributed more than half – 47 – including just three penalties.

Having already received Cambridgeshire County Youth recognition in the previous season, I made further County Youth appearances during 1977/1978 – enough to earn my 'colours'. There seems little doubt however, that this was as a direct result of my involvement with Cambridge City's first team, as opposed to my Sunday goal scoring exploits with Ely Crusaders under-18s.

At the end of the 1977/1978 season the players and officials associated with Ely Crusaders had a whip-round, and with the money raised we bought a white leather football and paid a sign-writer in Stretham to paint on it the following inscription: *"To 'Chic'. Manager of Ely Crusaders under-18s, Cambridge & District Sunday Youth League Champions 1977/1978."*

CHAPTER SEVEN: It was the best of times and the worst of times

Having been effectively dismissed by Cambridge City following the Munns Cup incident, I began pre-season training with Kings Lynn Football Club in the summer of 1978. I had to make my own way to 'The Walks' from Ely twice a week for training, and then for midweek and Saturday games too. I had not yet started full-time employment, so I guess that I was the only 'Linnets' player on the books who had recently thrown in his paper round!

Training was extraordinarily hard, but I definitely benefited as player-manager Keith Rudd put us through our paces. I had also developed physically from working on the farm with my dad during harvest time. Much of the time was occupied with straw-carting, an activity in which bales of straw were picked up individually on a pitchfork and 'pitched' on to a trailer. As the stack on the trailer grew, the bales had to be pitched higher and higher – and they were by no means light! By the time the trailer stack was complete, you literally had to jump and pitch the bale at the same time! The work was no easier when you took your turn on the trailer either; bales were being pitched at you from all directions, and you had to build the stack in a particular way or it would fall over: Two bales lengthways at the front (because of the metal struts on either side of the trailer), three lengthways behind those, two lengthways behind those and two side-ways, slightly overlapping the edge of the trailer. You then fitted two more in lengthways between those overlapping the edge, and moving backwards laid three more lengthways. When one level was completed, you stood on those snugly-fitted bales and started the whole process again with three more lengthways.

It was like building a solid house, and the only time you

got any respite was mid-morning when you went back to the farmhouse for some breakfast, mid-afternoon when you had a break for coffee and sandwiches, or when the baler broke down (which thank heavens, it frequently did!) Once the trailer stack was complete and you had it roped down ready for transport, you returned to the farm and decanted the bales to the large stack, usually throwing them by the strings which held them together. And off you went again with the empty trailer back to the field, until all the bales had been removed and stacked at the farm. You very seldom see the smaller rectangular bales of straw nowadays; instead the fields are full of gargantuan cylinder bales which are transported by fork lift devices or which can be rolled down the slopes to crush trespassers and unsuspecting wildlife. It saddens me to think that the young farmers of today are unlikely to experience the 'joys' of such labour-intensive straw-carting in the searing heat of harvest time.

1978/1979 happened to be Kings Lynn's centenary season, so our first three 'friendly' fixtures were all against Football League opposition – Cambridge United, Peterborough United and Aston Villa, all at home. The last of our six pre-season matches would be at home to Norwich City, by which time midfielder Clive Adams and striker Trevor Moden would have returned after a spell playing in Canada.

Adams broke his leg whilst abroad, but Moden was fit from his North American adventures and I was able to travel with him to training and to matches because he lived in Littleport, a town on the A10 five miles from Ely and on the way to Kings Lynn. It was still a lengthy journey and I was sometimes bundled into the back of the two-seat Triumph Spitfire, owing to the fact that a friend of Trevor's (who worked at the club) travelled too (and in truth, he was far too big to occupy anything but a seat in the car!)

I was quite good in the air – particularly for my height – but Moden was around six-foot-four and unbelievable. He was also an accomplished finisher, and had a spell with Nottingham Forest when apparently he was very highly thought of by no less a man than Brian Clough. Again though, Moden – despite all his obvious attributes – never played professionally either. I cannot believe that there were 92 better target men playing league football at the time in question.

I was very much looking forward to playing alongside 'Mo-Jo' (or 'Trebor' as I sometimes called him) and establishing the archetypal striking partnership - like Gilzean and Greaves, Toshack and Keegan, Jones and Clarke, O'Hare and Hector, Moden and Green (?). Player-manager Keith Rudd looked to be bringing his illustrious career to a close, and another new signing – Gary Mills – did not look quite the part in my opinion. The talented Jackie Gallagher was another striking option for Rudd, but he appeared to be on his way to signing professional forms for Lincoln City. Gallagher did make a Football League career for himself, but it was predominantly with Peterborough United instead.

When we trained on the 'Walks' pitch, one of our sessions involved a full-scale match, but one with a difference. Rudd said it would last only 20 minutes, and I soon found out why. When you passed the ball, you had to put yourself in a position to receive a return pass. That sounds simple enough, but if you had just made a 60-yard pass, your actions resulted in a 60-yard sprint! And in all likelihood, play had already moved on by the time you arrived at your destination. Clearly the object of the exercise was to encourage shorter, sharper passes, and also to make yourself available again for the return. The more options the player on the ball has, the better. So many players at lower levels pass the ball and then let their team-mate simply get on with it. They are either not 'educated' enough to know differently, or are not fit enough to maintain their involvement in the move – either receiving the ball back, or creating space by drawing opponents into areas they don't want to go. Unlike Worthington at Cambridge City, Rudd at least had some attributes as a coach. As far as I was concerned, all Worthington had going for him was the share of his famous brother's surname.

So we lined up for our first friendly match against Cambridge United, who fielded their best 11 players throughout the first half and then replaced them all for the start of the second period. The emerging striker Alan Biley scored one of United's two first half goals, and beanpole centre-half Steve Fallon gave me such a physical examination for 45 minutes that I still carry one of the scars on my left ankle to this very day. He was as hard as nails, and excellent in the air too.

Nevertheless, I just failed to connect with a Roy McManus cross on one occasion, and on another turned and shot powerfully wide from 20-yards. I thought I did OK, and the Lynn Advertiser reported the following day that I "looked as if I could be dangerous up front." Of United's team, Fallon quite clearly made an impression on me (!), but the player who really caught my eye was Peter Sylvester. He had enjoyed a productive career at Norwich City, and although he was now in his twilight years he still had the most exquisite touch.

The score remained 2-0 until the final whistle, and if the news reporter had marked my performance out of 10, I think I would have deserved a six. In the 1-0 defeat against Peterborough United I felt I was rather less effective, but it was still early days and I had the mouth-watering clash with Aston Villa to look forward to. It turned out to be perhaps the best performance of my entire career.

Villa sent over a young side, but a number of their players were soon to be part of a League Championship winning side, and then European Cup winners the following season, courtesy of a 1-0 victory over Bayern Munich. Goalkeeper Nigel Spink, centre-halves Allan Evans and Colin Gibson, and striker Gary Shaw were all players who went on to forge international careers to some degree or another.

Gibson – subsequently acquired by Manchester United – was my marker in the Villa game, and I felt that I gave him a pretty torrid time. As the Lynn Advertiser remarked afterwards, I showed "speed and aggression." On this day, for Gibson – who must have been around the same age as me – it seemed that I had too much of both.

Midway through the first period, Rudd and I broke into the Villa half and it was two-against-two. Rudd had possession, and although Gibson was tracking me as I approached the penalty area, I called for the ball and the player-manager delivered. I was now 15 yards from the centre of the goal, with only Gibson and Spink to beat. After receiving the ball on my left foot, I knocked it a yard to the right and in the same movement delivered a crisp, rising shot which flew past the goalkeeper's left hand. The Lynn Advertiser mentioned that "it was a particularly good one," and it certainly was. Gibson had been left flat-footed and the promising Spink was given absolutely no chance by the ferocity of the shot.

That goal separated the teams at half-time, but Villa improved after the break and managed to get back on level terms. We subsequently won a penalty kick which I would gladly have taken, but the spot-kick – twice-taken by Freddie Easthall – was saved identically on both occasions by Spink.

A few moments later however, we were back in front.

Gallagher received the ball wide on the left, but was closely attended. I made a run down the middle, and when Gallagher saw this he beat his man and delivered a low, hard cross to the edge of the area. Spink had spotted the danger and was advancing quickly from his line, but I reached the ball first with my right foot and guided it about a yard to the left, away from his reach. I was challenged simultaneously by a defender, but managed to withstand his last-ditch effort and glide the ball into an empty net, making it 2-1.

I was ecstatic, and celebrated wildly. Future England international Shaw capitalised on late Villa pressure to grab an opportunistic equaliser, but this had been my day in the limelight – I had scored twice against mighty Aston Villa! But my performance that day wasn't just about the goals, and I wondered if the future England under-21 and Manchester United defender Gibson had ever had a tougher examination of his football credentials at that stage of his career.

When the game finished, I was elated. I pictured the goals over and over in my mind, and wondered if perhaps the Villa management had seen any potential in me. If Gibson and Spink – both about the same age as me – were first team material, why wasn't I?

But Villa never came knocking. In hindsight, I wish I had approached them instead, but I honestly believed that if they had been watching the same game that I had just played in, they would at least consider giving me a trial. Perhaps they thought I did not have the attributes to develop like Spink, Gibson and Shaw, but surely any player has the potential to get better? It wasn't as if I had capitalised on sloppy defending; I had created and scored two really good goals. Was I not worth a second glance?

It is possible that a degree of complacency may have set in

after the euphoria of the Villa game, because I did not fare so well in the subsequent friendly draws with Diss Town (2-2) and Ely City (0-0). I did however, score a well-taken penalty to salvage the home draw in the first of those games.

Our final pre-season match was against Norwich City, and with Moden now back in the reckoning there was more competition for places. I didn't think I did too badly in a goalless first half, but was substituted at the interval and goals from Moden and my replacement Mills secured a 2-0 win.

The first competitive fixture of the season for Kings Lynn was a First Round Southern League Cup tie against non-league giants Kettering Town, to be played over two legs. I was (and felt I deserved to be) in the starting line-up, and eagerly anticipated a meeting with one of the best teams operating outside the Football League. Almost immediately, I had the chance to make my mark. Former West Bromwich Albion full-back Lyndon Hughes left his back-pass short and I was on to it in a flash, with just the goalkeeper to beat.

Now I never had a pre-ordained method when it came to a one-on-one with the goalkeeper. Sometimes I shot early, and sometimes I shot late or tried to round the 'keeper. Whenever I shot, it was usually for the corners. Perhaps if I was lacking form or confidence I would simply blast it and hope for the best, but generally speaking I tried to place the ball home. I have never understood the match commentators praising strikers when they blast the ball goalwards and it 'happens' to go through the goalkeeper's legs. Whenever that happened to me, I never felt pleased with the quality of my finishing, because it owed everything to luck and virtually nothing to skill. Blasting a penalty kick is much the same thing – surely good players can place the ball pretty much where they want, no matter how hard they strike it?

In my entire career, I only once deliberately 'nutmegged' the goalkeeper. It was in a match at Haverhill Rovers FC for Cambridge Taxes against arch-rivals Leicester Taxes. I managed to intercept a pass on the halfway line and then nodded the ball forward as I sped towards goal. I knew the Leicester 'keeper was useful, and it came as no surprise to me when he didn't go to ground prematurely. With my angles rapidly narrowing, I decided for the first time ever that the best route to goal was through his legs, so that is where I successfully placed the ball. We lost 4-1, but in my view the 'nutmegging' issue is an important one. The best strikers are not content with merely 'getting it on target'; they put the ball inside the post or underneath the crossbar. Jimmy Greaves is the name that immediately springs to mind in that respect. He was the supreme finisher.

Anyway, when my chance came against Kettering, I was thwarted by the goalkeeper. He stood his ground, and when I tried to round him on the right he stuck out his left hand and succeeded in stopping the ball. That proved to be just about the only chance we had, and Kettering crushed us 4-0 with future Chelsea star Billy Kellock in particular giving us the proverbial runaround.

I was relegated to substitute for the return leg (which we lost 3-0), and was 12th man again for the opening league game at home to Merthyr Tydfil which we lost by the same scoreline. Suddenly, from being the star of the show against Aston Villa, I was being criticised in training for the 'body-shape' I adopted when receiving and controlling the ball. There were perhaps many things about me that the management could have criticised and sought to improve, but my ball control wasn't one of them.

I next found myself in the Reserves for the 1-0 defeat at

home to Spalding Reserves, whilst player-manager Rudd and Easthall found the net in a 2-1 victory against Bury Town in the FA Cup First Qualifying Round. I will never know if Rudd's first goal of the 1978/1979 season prompted him to believe that he could prolong his already noteworthy career, but at the next training session he informed me that I was now surplus to his requirements.

I was devastated. In nine pre-season and competitive matches, Kings Lynn FC had scored six goals and I had scored half of them – including the double against Aston Villa. So what had this 18-year old done so badly wrong? From believing I was on top of the tree with a great performance against Villa, I now found myself six feet (or should I say five-feet nine inches) below the roots of that very same tree.

CHAPTER EIGHT: No longer indestructible

Inevitably perhaps, I made my way back to Ely City hoping to re-build my career and my self-confidence, and I followed a fruitless 2-0 league defeat at Wisbech Town with three goals in successive cup ties. Clacton Town were beaten 4-0 away in the FA Cup (for which I was eligible, having missed the Kings Lynn v Bury Town tie), and Peterborough League side Leverington Sports were dispatched 3-0 in the FA Vase before we suffered another 2-0 league defeat at home to Gorleston.

High-flying Lowestoft Town were the next visitors to the 'Paradise' Ground in the FA Cup, and for a reason I cannot remember I started the match as substitute. I was introduced at half-time – which suggests that there may have been no sinister reason for my original exclusion – and we were trailing by two goals towards the finish when I collected the ball about 35-yards from goal. Moving slightly infield, I unleashed a swerving left-foot shot into the top left-hand corner which the goalkeeper could only watch. Graham Duguid was then denied by the 'keeper as we pushed forward for the equaliser, but Lowestoft held on in the end for a 2-1 win.

In the Ely Standard newspaper, the then player-manager Roger Pauley was quoted along the following lines: "He (me) scores one of the best goals ever seen at the 'Paradise' and then goes and gets himself injured in a Sunday League game."

The incident he was referring to was my clash with the Hinton Rangers goalkeeper in the Ely Crusaders Senior Division fixture the day after my Lowestoft goal. We had started the Sunday season well, and it seemed clear that this particular teenager was capable of having a major influence on the team's fortunes in the top flight of

Cambridgeshire Sunday football.

I had struck twice in the opening day 3-1 win against Linton Sunday, and after missing out on our 6-0 thrashing by Littlebury I was back for the 3-2 victory against Burwell-based Queens Arms. Next came the return clash with Littlebury, and this marked the beginning of a quite 'beautiful' relationship between myself and the Essex-based club. I think I can quite honestly say that almost single-handedly, I prevented that particular team from ever winning the Sunday League title, despite for many years being perhaps the best side in it.

In my first encounter with Littlebury, we were trailing by two goals at the break and at that point in time they probably felt capable of repeating the 6-0 win they had recorded on their own patch against us. I pulled one back from the penalty spot at the start of the second half, but the visitors soon restored their two-goal advantage and must have believed they were cruising to another comfortable win. Ian Smith then fed me from the left wing and I dragged a left-foot shot into the far corner of the net to make it 2-3. Then something quite extraordinary happened. It was as if Littlebury had suddenly become petrified by a single player. They passed the ball a couple of times from the subsequent restart, but – unaware of any team-mates around me – I immediately intercepted one of the passes and advanced forward before placing a low 20-yard shot into the corner of the net to earn a 3-3 draw.

Forward in time and back at Cherry Hinton, I had chased a ball into the heart of the Hinton Rangers penalty area late in the first half. The goalkeeper caught it and stood firm for my approach. We collided, shoulder-to-shoulder, but something snapped near my neck. I tried to 'wheel' my arm, but it was agony and I knew it was bad. It later emerged that I had suffered a 'green-stick' fracture of the left collar-bone, so I was immediately out of action.

I returned – perhaps prematurely – for Ely Crusaders at Linton, finding the net twice in a 3-1 win, and I was on target the following week at Selser, where we established a 2-0 interval lead. Unfortunately however, I broke my collar-bone again in a 60th minute collision with Selser's man-mountain defender Nigel Lawrence, and after my departure we conceded three goals to go down 3-2.

Side-lined again, I watched helplessly as my Senior Division team-mates lost eight of their final nine league matches, scoring only seven times and conceding 43. In fairness I did play in the penultimate fixture at home to champions Phoenix which – having incredibly lost to them 11-0 the week before – we lost by a 9-0 margin as the quicksilver Terry Rider tore us to shreds once more.

I did return briefly for Ely City, introduced as a 70th minute substitute in the 0-0 draw at Stowmarket. In the fourth game of my 'come-back' against Haverhill Rovers however, I tore a hamstring, prompting me to announce that my season was over. In fact I did play a few late-season games and scored three times in tour matches in Holland and Germany, but – other than the high of my two-goal burst against Aston Villa – the 1978/1979 season was one that I simply wished to forget – except for one thing.

On 16 September 1978, I commenced full-time employment with the Inland Revenue, thus affirming my status as a bastard. So before the aforementioned series of injuries curtailed my season, I had the opportunity to make my mark on the Revenue football scene.

Playing for Cambridge Taxes, I led the forward line alongside Saffron Walden and Linton Granta target man Dave Christie. We shared 12 goals between the two of us in successive 7-0 Somerset House Cup victories before travelling down to play London Taxes at the Civil Service

Sports Ground at Barnes Bridge near Chiswick, on the banks of the River Thames. I didn't know it at the time, but this venue would become very familiar to me in the 17 or so years that followed.

Cambridge Taxes, having trailed 3-2 at half-time, established a 5-3 second half lead and I had scored four times. This had not gone unnoticed by Don Cain, a member of the London Taxes team and Treasurer for the Great Britain & Northern Ireland representative side. With a semi-final place seemingly within our grasp, Scottish centre-half and Union activist Tom 'head-butt' Hedley decided to live up to his nickname and was dismissed from the field. London responded with three goals in quick succession to clinch the tie 6-5, but in terms of getting noticed by the right people, my job was done.

The Somerset House Cup was contested by individual offices throughout the British Isles, but when the format of that competition changed and was subsequently replaced by the less romantically named Regional Competition, individual office teams in the Eastern Counties were able to compete for a new trophy – the Hoadley Cup. Leicester Taxes won this cup most often, but in 1990/1991 Cambridge Taxes beat them on the way to the final, which we won 1-0 against Yarmouth Taxes with a goal from Glyn Carroll.

Under the management of Peter Reece, Cambridge Taxes reached the 1991/1992 final as well, meeting Aylesbury in the final at Rushden & Diamonds' old ground. Again we won 1-0 – this time when Nick Wells scored with his knee – but I got clattered by the goalkeeper just before the final whistle. Consequently I am missing from most of the post-match team photos, because I was busy knocking on house doors outside the ground, trying to find someone who would let me have a bag of frozen peas to put on my dead-leg! I managed to get some as well!

Talking of Peter Reece, I remember a game we were playing against Norwich Taxes at Cherry Hinton. Some of the Inspectors from the Cambridge Tax Office came to watch, and when the half-time whistle sounded we were only 1-0 up, courtesy of my header. Well, during the interval, 'Reecy' came out with the most foul-mouthed tirade I have ever heard from a manager – either before, at the time, or since. The watching Inspectors stood open-mouthed in a state of shock, and so did we! It worked though; I scored five more in the second half, and we eventually won the match 10-0!

CHAPTER NINE: Emerging from the doldrums

Excluding the comparatively meaningless 10 goals scored for Cambridge Taxes and the three end-of-season tour goals in Holland and Germany, my injury-blighted 1978/1979 season had yielded only a handful of goals; three in the 'friendlies' for Kings Lynn, three in cup matches for Ely City and eight (albeit at a rate of more than a goal-per-game) for Ely Crusaders in the Sunday League Senior Division, where we just managed to avoid relegation. Only the slightly poorer records of both NERA and Linton Sunday saved us from the drop, and David Clarke's tenure as Crusaders manager was mercifully ended.

He was replaced by former Youth Team boss 'Chic' Cooper. His first challenge, involving many of the players he had been so successful with at youth level, came with the club's first ever entry into the Sunday League six-a-side tournament at Longstanton. Our 1979 line-up consisted of goalkeeper Roger Smith, defenders Richard Goodjohn and Pat Hennebry, midfielders Ian Smith and Gary Chilvers, with me as the lone striker. All six players also played for Ely City at one stage or another of their careers.

We were unbeaten in our group games, and didn't concede a single goal. We knew things would get tougher in the quarter-finals however, and we were held to a 0-0 draw by one of the two sides fielded by Senior Division rivals Girton Eagles. The penalty shoot-out went our way though, earning a semi-final meeting with the other Girton Eagles team. Again it finished goalless, and again penalties were required to separate the teams. We were still level after five spot-kicks each, but our goalkeeper Roger managed to block Girton's sixth penalty with his face. This left him extremely dazed and sporting a black eye, and his next task was to fire us into the final of the competition against his opposite number. After recovering his composure he managed to do so with aplomb, so we were through to the final!

Selser awaited us after this dramatic victory, and it transpired that we had reserved our best form for that match. Ian Smith took a throw-in midway through the first period, and I side-stepped prickly midfielder Mick Iwanko before crashing in a great shot past Richard Powis off the underside of the bar – my sixth goal of the tournament – to put us in front.

Selser never really threatened to equalise, and we made the game safe after the break. I managed to flick on a through ball past the last defender, and Ian ran on to crack a superb drive in off the foot of the left-hand post to make the final score 2-0. Our young team had won the competition without conceding a goal, but as it turned out this was not the start of an era of unbridled success for Ely Crusaders (particularly that is, if success is measured in terms of silverware). But as I said in my interview with the Cambridge Evening News Light Blue* afterwards, we had at least showed the Sunday League that teams from outside Cambridge could play a bit too.

> *The football edition of the Cambridge Evening News was printed immediately after five o'clock on a Saturday, when all the football matches had finished, and it was coloured light blue. Apart from reporting on matches that had occurred on the day however, it also included articles about Cambridgeshire Sunday and midweek football.*

After the catastrophes that had otherwise befallen me during the 1978/1979 season, I had become disenchanted with Saturday football. Disillusioned, having failed to make the grade at Kings Lynn, my bitterness was compounded one afternoon towards the end of that season when – whilst standing in the crowd watching an Ely City match – I happened to meet Lynn manager Keith Rudd again. He said that in hindsight he had been far too hasty in letting me go, but as I was now injured anyway there was nothing he could do to rectify the situation. The 'Linnets' did not fare too well that season, and my young potential had perhaps been too easily discarded.

All of that was consigned to history as the 1979/1980 campaign got underway, and I made the decision to play Sunday football only. Ely Crusaders then proceeded to have the best league season in their history, challenging for the Senior Division title alongside the usual protagonists Phoenix and our bitter not-so-local rivals Littlebury.

Noticing that I was no longer involved in Saturday football, County League side Sutton United – a village team based six miles from Ely – made an enquiry for me. I knew many of the players through my time at Crusaders, so I decided to sign and made my debut at Cambridge-based Pye (later to become Philips in the world of telecommunications). Without going into too much detail, I scored six times on my debut in a 9-1 win, and in the next six league and cup games I increased my goal tally to 12. It was all too easy. Mind you, Sutton had many other useful players too, none more so than Alan Moore who remained one of my local favourites. In my view he was a player who had everything, and could play anywhere (except in goal maybe).

In the last of my Sutton appearances at Waterbeach I fell heavily on my shoulder again, and although the collar-bone had not broken it was bad enough to keep me out for a few games. My footballing 'renaissance' prompted Ely City to put in an approach for me, so I made the decision to return to the 'Robins'. When I re-signed, player-manager Lester Newell made it clear that he would never entertain me again if I left to go and play village football!

I returned to the Town & Country League (as it was then known) with our only goal in a 3-1 defeat at Haverhill Rovers. I was then on target again as Newell scored twice in the 3-0 home victory over Braintree & Crittall Athletic, but came off with 15 minutes remaining in the 1-1 draw at Stowmarket Town and was then missing for the same result at home to Yarmouth Town. I was on as late substitute for the next two matches at Colchester United Reserves and Saffron Walden – also draws – before coming on with 15 minutes of normal time remaining in the home League Cup semi-final clash with Clacton Town. We trailed 2-0 at the break, but Trevor Moden – now an Ely City player having also left Kings Lynn – pulled one back prior to my introduction. Time was running out however, so when a free-kick was awarded in our favour play was stopped and I sprinted on to the field. I ran into the Clacton penalty area as the free-kick was delivered, and without breaking stride suddenly found the ball at my feet. Side-footing home, I made the scores level at last and there were no further goals in extra-time.

I was back in favour for the league visit to Gorleston, scoring with a diving header and striking the post immediately afterwards before we went down 3-1 to the reigning champions.

Several weeks later we had the League Cup semi-final replay at Clacton, which – unusually – was played on a Sunday. This meant that once again I had to choose between my Saturday club and my Sunday club Ely Crusaders, who were playing away at Hinton Rangers. On this occasion however – with Crusaders having nothing to play for but pride – it made sense to opt for the Ely City match. That was something of a novelty – me making a decision based on common sense.

At Crusaders, we had opened our 1979/1980 Senior Division campaign with an exhilarating 4-3 victory at Queens Arms (which proved to be the only time we ever defeated them on their own patch). I drilled home the low angled winner with my left foot as we came from 3-2 down at the break to win by the odd goal in seven. That win looked even more remarkable 14 days later, when we travelled to Burwell again to take on Queens Arms in the League Cup. Having been on level terms 2-2 at half-time, we somehow contrived to lose 8-2 as our goalkeeper Roger Smith endured something of a second half nightmare! Goals were flying into our net from every conceivable angle, including direct from a corner-kick!

Powerful Phoenix were our next opponents in the league, and for once we totally outplayed them, with Moden – now an Ely Sunday recruit too – and myself finding the net. Phoenix however, had the left-footed goal-scoring phenomenon Terry Rider in their ranks, and he scored from the only three chances that came his way to leave us empty-handed. Terry like me was a Civil Servant, working for the Ministry of Agriculture Farming & Fisheries. He therefore played up front for Agricola in the Lewis Cup, but the Inland Revenue – being a much bigger department – was always much too strong for them.

St Andrews next visited Downham Road in the Sunday League, and I accounted for half of the goals in a 6-0 win. I then grabbed our only goal in a 1-1 draw at Barnwell before the successive visits to Ely of Hinton Rangers and Girton Eagles. The Hinton right-back was one of the diminutive Tully twins who used to play for Manorians – a team we had thrashed regularly at Youth level – so with that in mind he adopted an approach towards me which could loosely be described as 'over-zealous'.

I looped in a goal which Tully made it apparent he considered to be "lucky", and this was cancelled out by the visitors to leave it 1-1 at the midway point. I was causing Tully increasing difficulty as the second half wore on, so as I took the ball past him on the left he aimed a kick at me which I managed to avoid completely. I ran forward with the ball and he delivered another foul which this time clipped me, but still I remained on my feet. His final attempt to ground me was a full-blooded scythe, and although this made me stumble I still remained upright. Referee Malcolm Pick had seen enough however, and ordered Tully from the field.

As Tully trudged off, the Hinton Rangers manager informed him in no uncertain terms that he had played his last game for the club.

I was on target again as we ran out 5-1 winners, but the following week we discovered that someone had taken a car and skidded all over the wet Downham Road pitch, leaving deep ruts and rendering it totally unplayable. I'll never know who was responsible, but it seemed a bit strange after what had happened the previous Sunday.

The following week we had to entertain highly-fancied Girton Eagles, but on the City of Ely College pitch instead. They could not cope with Moden however, and he contributed a hat-trick to our emphatic 4-1 success. I was on the scoresheet too, meaning that I had scored in all six of our league games to date. Two more goals followed for me in the 4-2 Sunday Challenge Cup defeat at Hinton Rangers, and a subsequent 2-1 defeat at Selser marked my first league game without a goal, and emphasised the fact that Crusaders were nowhere near as effective away from home.

Next came Littlebury back at our Downham Road pitch, but we trailed 1-0 at the break and had it all to do in the second half. I equalised with a thumping header however, and in the last minute followed up Moden's blocked shot to grab a dramatic 2-1 winner.

In the New Year Girton Eagles avenged their 4-1 loss by edging us out 2-1 on their own patch, but we did the very same to Selser the following week on their visit to Ely, with Gary Chilvers scoring twice including a 40-yard thunderbolt. I was then back on the goal-trail with four in the 13-1 demolition of bottom club St Andrews, and as a result Ely Crusaders went top of the Sunday League for the first and only time in their history. The next few matches would be crucial, with visits to our nearest challengers Littlebury and Phoenix, who both had games in hand of us.

A late Terry Rider goal denied us the point we deserved at Phoenix, and the same 1-0 scoreline saw us go down at Littlebury the week after I had scored the winner in the 2-1 defeat of Barnwell. By this stage of the season the team's injuries were mounting up, and we next faced Sawston Keys at home with a severely depleted line-up. I managed to bundle the ball home for the only goal of the first half, but we had been outplayed and almost inevitably found ourselves trailing 5-1 before I struck again with a diving header. I then tore a hamstring late on, but all that did was compound the misery of a title challenge which had been derailed by three defeats in four outings. The lads rallied by completing the league double over Queens Arms and winning 1-0 at Sawston Keys, but it was too little too late and the best we could do was to finish a respectable third behind champions Phoenix and runners-up Littlebury.

So with the Sunday League title beyond our reach, I missed the aforementioned trip to Hinton Rangers (which Crusaders lost 3-1) and travelled instead to Clacton for the Town & Country League Cup semi-final replay. The match proved to be a Johnny Fretwell master-class, as he opened the scoring in the first half before defender Ray Brown wrapped up a rather comfortable 2-0 win after the break to put us into the final against hot favourites Lowestoft Town.

We gleaned only a point from our next four league outings, but I scored in the final league game – a 2-0 win at Brantham Athletic – and was therefore disappointed to be left out of the starting line-up for the first leg of the League Cup final at Lowestoft's Crown Meadow. Second half goals from Peter Speed and Trevor Moden seemed to justify Lester Newell's decision to exclude me, but I was back for the second leg in Ely owing to a John Edwards injury. We took the lead, but were trailing 2-1 when I made what could have been a catastrophic back-pass. It went straight to the feet of Lowestoft centre-forward Tony Cheek, but with the goal at his mercy he dragged his shot wide of the far post and I breathed a huge sigh of relief as we went straight up the other end to score again and clinch the tie 4-2 on aggregate.

The Town & Country League Cup remains to this day, the only major competition ever won by the 'Robins'.

CHAPTER TEN: A Century of Goals

It is my firm belief that within the space of three seasons, I played for arguably the best team in Ely City's history, and then possibly the worst.

Buoyed by the League Cup success of 1979/1980, player-manager Lester Newell proceeded to assemble a squad which contained an unrivalled array of striking talent. There was Moden of course, recapturing his best form to terrorise defences with his aerial threat and clinical finishing; Burnley-bred Gary Grogan, a languid playmaker who was later to become Cambridge City's all-time leading goalscorer; John 'Soapy' Edwards, an enigmatic dead-ball-specialising winger who could fascinate and frustrate in equal measure, and of course there was the 20-year old Steve 'Midge' Green.

Even Newell – a former classy centre-forward himself – defied the advancing years by virtue of a lithe build and a keen eye for goal from midfield. He also had the luxury of being able to deploy Johnny Fretwell's striking attributes at full-back, pre-empting the modern-day wing-back in a fluid and forward-looking formation.

Goals also came from elsewhere in the team. Deeper-lying midfielder Ted Robbins and tackle-hungry Bob Lyon popped up with the odd contribution, and defenders on target during 1980/1981 included full-backs Peter Stearman and Peter Galenski, along with central defenders Ray Brown, Roger Crane and Pat Hennebry.

With so many attacking options at Newell's disposal, I initially found myself on the substitute bench as City drew 0-0 away to title favourites Sudbury Town, and won 1-0 at Histon courtesy of a second half goal from Edwards. I then came on with eight minutes remaining as Edwards and Moden struck in the 2-1 win at Saffron Walden Town, and with 25 minutes left in the 6-0 humbling of Histon in which Moden (4) and Grogan (2) shared the spoils.

My first start of the campaign came at Braintree & Crittall Athletic, and I got the opportunity to break the deadlock when we were awarded a second half penalty. My tame effort was easily saved by the goalkeeper, but moments later Newell broke free near the right-hand goal-line and when he cut the ball back to the near post I was on hand to score with a rising side-foot half-volley. 'Soapy' Edwards made the points safe with a well-taken second, and we suddenly found ourselves unbeaten and top of the table.

Fierce Fenland rivals Wisbech Town were our next opponents the following Tuesday night, and I thought I would miss the kick-off because my lift from Cambridge to Ely was delayed. The players were all out on the pitch warming up by the time I arrived, so I only just had time to get changed before the referee signalled the start of the match. Seconds later however, he was whistling again – this time following a goal from me.

Ian 'Jigger' Jones was a tigerish defender for Wisbech, and I had encountered him on many occasions in the past. In one particular clash between Needhams School Ely and Wisbech Grammar, I recall that the two of us largely ignored the ball and proceeded instead to kick proverbial lumps out of each other.

As soon as the Ely City v Wisbech Town clash got underway, 'Jigger' and I soon found ourselves in close proximity tussling for the ball. He somehow injured his hip in the challenge however, and I moved forward to hook a left-foot drive inside the far post to give us the lead. 'Jigger' had to depart from the action, and in his absence Wisbech's defence was literally shredded by Moden, Grogan and myself as we ran out 7-0 winners. I struck again with a smart shot on the turn but Moden was unstoppable, helping himself to a hat-trick as Grogan and Newell chipped in with a goal-a-piece.

I scored again as Thetford Town were dispatched 3-1 away from home, and then for a fourth consecutive game as we silenced Wisbech's Fenland Park* faithful with an emphatic 3-0 win. I grabbed the only goal of the second half and it was one of my best of the season, a dipping volley from 30-yards which soared into the top right-hand corner of the net. Few teams – if any – have beaten Wisbech twice in a season by an aggregate of 10-0.

> *I'll always remember the fact that former Watford, AC Milan and England striker Luther Blissett was once asked about the most intimidating ground he had ever played at. Was it the San Siro? The Stadio Olimpico? The Stadio delle Alpi? Hampden Park? The Den? No, as far as he was concerned it was Fenland Park!*

I was missing through injury as the 'Robins' hit seven again, this time at the expense of Felixstowe Town who did at least manage a consolation goal. Either side of that we suffered 1-0 cup defeats at Corby Town in the FA Cup, and at Hoddesdon Town in the FA Vase. I was also absent for the 1-1 league draw at Colchester United Reserves and the home win against Haverhill Rovers, when Edwards grabbed the only goal of the game. So after 11 league games, we were still top of the table on 20 points (two points for a win), having scored 33 goals and conceded just four.

For Ely Crusaders on Sundays, things were not going quite so well. I was present for the opening two defeats – 1-0 at Hinton Rangers and 2-0 at home to Littlebury, but I was absent for the 2-1 defeat at Blades and the 3-1 defeat at Queens Arms, either side of a home 2-2 draw against Phoenix in which I did find the net. I was goalkeeper for

75 minutes as we slipped to a 2-1 defeat at Sawston Keys, but after helping myself to four in the 5-1 League Cup defeat of Bar Hill I was back in scoring league action at home to Selser, where again we had to settle for a point from a 2-2 draw.

I struck for the third consecutive league game after coming on as substitute against a severely depleted Sawston Keys outfit and we claimed our first league success of the season by a flattering 7-1 margin, but I was out again for the visit to Selser and the 3-0 defeat left us at the foot of the table with only four points from nine outings, and only another nine games remaining to pull our nuts out of the fire.

At Ely City meanwhile we suffered our first league reverse of the campaign going down 2-0 at Brantham Athletic, but our next fixture was a home encounter with the youngsters from Colchester United Reserves and what a match that proved to be.

I nodded in our opener after we had gone two goals down, and 'Soapy' was also on target as we trailed 3-2 at the break. Colchester restored their two-goal advantage in the second period, but I side-footed home to reduce the arrears and then completed my hat-trick with a close-range volley to make the final score 4-4. The headline in the Ely Standard newspaper the following week read: *'Green trio holds Bunkell* babes.'*

   * *Colchester stalwart Ray Bunkell was the Colchester United Reserves manager.*

Our next league match was a 5-1 home win against Chatteris Town, sandwiched by a two-legged cup tie which involved the previous season's league and league cup winners – Gorleston and ourselves – which we proceeded to lose 5-1 on aggregate.

Moden was on target in the 2-2 league draw at Clacton Town, and by this time had helped himself to a total of 16 goals – all in the league. A shock 1-0 home defeat by County League Great Shelford in the Cambs Invitation Cup was unexpected, but we were soon back on the goal trail in the Town & Country League, hammering Chatteris Town 6-0 away and Stowmarket Town 3-0 at home, where I grabbed my ninth league goal of the season.

We lost yet another cup match – this time 2-1 at Newmarket Town as we fell at the first hurdle in our defence of the Town & Country League Cup – but at least were able to embark on the rest of the season without the distraction of any knock-out competitions!

My tenth league goal of the campaign – another header – helped us defeat Braintree 5-2 at home, but we took only one point from our next four games and that severely dented our title ambitions. I was either substitute or missing for the next five matches which yielded three wins and two defeats, but returned to score in the 4-1 win at home to Newmarket and was subsequently a scoring substitute in the 4-0 home win over Clacton which stretched our unbeaten run to six. My 14th and final league goal of the season came in the 3-2 loss at Felixstowe, and this precipitated a run of 12 games which produced only three wins and three defeats.

That run dropped us to fourth in the table, but in the final game at Haverhill a second half equaliser from 'Soapy' accounted for our 100th league goal of the campaign. This was no mean feat in the days when players could pass the ball back to the goalkeeper without the fear of him doing anything more risky than simply picking it up!

My early season goal scoring exploits for City earned me a call-up for the Cambridgeshire County Senior team, and on my debut in the friendly against a Cambridge United XI at the Abbey Stadium I felt I excelled myself in a 3-0 win, making two of the goals. I was therefore selected to play against Nottinghamshire in the Inter-County Cup competition at the same venue, but inexplicably ate a doner kebab on the afternoon before the game and consequently felt dreadful, thus bringing down the curtain on my County career via a half-time substitution! Having made a lifetime habit of never eating anything before a match, I will never know what made me do so on this particular occasion – and why a bloody kebab for heaven's sake?

The only other time I broke my sacred rule of not eating before a game was when I travelled to Portsmouth to make my solitary appearance for the Civil Service representative side against The Royal Navy. The Civil Service – much like the Cambridgeshire County side – was selected on the basis of club status rather than known ability, and the team was predominantly chosen from the upper echelons of non-league football. So despite performing with distinction for the Inland Revenue Football Club year after year, I never looked remotely like getting the opportunity to face any of the Armed Forces.

However, on this particular occasion I got the call up (presumably because they were short of players), and travelled down to London before catching the coach to Portsmouth with my team-mates, including Inland Revenue strike partner Paul Patey. We arrived at the hotel, and milled around for a while before a very attractive waitress approached me and asked me how I would like it. In different circumstances (particularly given her outfit) I would have said in the nearest available bedroom, but I chose to apologise instead.

"Sorry?"

"How would you like it?" she repeated.

"Like what?"

"Your steak."

Finally I realised that she was asking me about the degree to which I would like some meat cooked.

"Medium-rare please."

So before – potentially – one of the most important games of my life, I was about to tuck into a juicy sirloin. "What the hell?" I thought. The chances of me being in this position again were somewhere between zero and remote, so I might as well make the most of it. Having ruined my County career with a doner kebab, I felt that I might as well scupper my Civil Service representative hopes with the flesh of some other unsuspecting animal.

When the meal was finished, I felt in no condition to play football. It was perhaps fortunate therefore, that I was named as substitute. The Navy clash was pretty dire, and I felt that I had played both with and against players who were far superior to those on show. Patey took a knock in the first half, and when he limped off at the interval my chance came.

The portion of deceased cow was fully digested by this time, so I was medium-raring to go when the second half got underway. To my surprise, the Navy team were not very good. Mind you, I didn't think that my own team were up to much either, so my efforts seemed unlikely to bear fruit. With less than a minute remaining however, my marker – who seemed quite disturbed by my mobility and ball control – allowed a long clearance to skid underneath his foot and behind the last line of defence. I was clear on goal.

Under normal circumstances I would have attempted to

score, but as I approached the box one of my team-mates called manically for the ball. With the goalkeeper at his near post and on the assumption that my vociferous teammate was unmarked in the middle, I decided to unselfishly square the ball into his path for a simple tap-in. To my dismay however, he was fully 25-yards from goal and was preceded by a defender, who simply tapped the ball back to his goalkeeper (which was allowed in those days) to avert the danger. That was one occasion when I wish I had shot rather than passed!

In the Navy clubhouse after the game, I pointed out to the Civil Service management team that whilst I could successfully make it by train from Portsmouth to Cambridge, I was unable to get a connection to Ely. I therefore asked for £15 to pay for a taxi from Cambridge to Ely. What happened next will come as no surprise to anyone who has worked for the Civil Service, but may come as a shock to people who have even the remotest shred of common sense.

"The Civil Service Sports Association rules state that we cannot pay for taxis," said the official as he guarded a pile of paper money nearly a foot high. "We are however, authorised to reimburse the costs of an overnight stay in a hotel up to the sum of £50."

"I just need to get back to Ely," I protested, "and the cost of a taxi will be far less than the cost of staying in a hotel."

"I'm sorry," said the official, "but rules are rules. We cannot pay taxi fares."

"OK then," I said, "I'll stay at a hotel in Cambridge."

"How much will that cost?" he asked.

"I don't know...£45?"

"OK, here you are."

And with that he handed me £45 from the large pile of notes, which I had already guessed represented more of a – ahem – financial inducement to my semi-professional colleagues to participate in the match as opposed to a legitimate reimbursement of expenses incurred.

Back on the domestic front, Ely City's gradual demise in the Town & Country League title race was in sharp contrast to the steep revival by Ely Crusaders in the Senior Division of the Sunday League. Although at Crusaders we had gleaned only four points from a possible 18 at the midway point of the 1980/1981 season, we had suffered just one league defeat at home – the opening 2-0 reverse at the hands of Littlebury. That was pretty much in line with the form we had shown in the previous campaign, when we had taken 14 points from a possible 18 on our own patch (winning seven times and losing just two) and in 1978/1979 when all 11 of the points we salvaged were on home soil.

In 1980/1981, five of our remaining nine fixtures were at Downham Road, so that was at least a crumb of comfort to us. Hinton Rangers were the first visitors, and a rare Ian Smith double helped us on the way to a 4-1 success. I opened the scoring with a good header as Melbourn-based Blades were dispatched 3-1 at the same venue, but (if the goalkeeping appearance at Sawston Keys is not taken into account) my run of seven successive scoring appearances in all competitions came to a halt in a noteworthy 2-2 draw at Phoenix.

I was back on the scoresheet as Soham Town Rangers were dispatched 3-2, and I grabbed a well-taken hat-trick in the 4-4 draw at Girton Eagles before notching again in the 3-0 win at Soham and in a 3-2 success at Littlebury. This gave me a total of 16 goals in 12 outfield appearances, and at last we were safe from the spectre of relegation. My second goal in the draw at Girton was one of my favourites, as I outfoxed Ely City team-mate Peter Galenski on the edge of his own penalty area. He was shadowing me when I ran on to a through-ball down the middle, but I cut the ball back inside him with my right foot and with the outside of the same foot curled a delicious shot just inside the left-hand post.

The game at Littlebury was an odd one. The pitch was rock hard due to frost, and in the current Health & Safety climate I cannot believe that the game would ever have taken place. It was quite a long trip for us however, so the referee decided that if the players were sensible, the match could go ahead. Clearly he was not aware of the history between the two sides! It was a proverbial skating rink, but we adapted better than the hosts and established a 2-0 lead before my shot was deflected in for our third.

Littlebury pulled a couple of goals back near the finish, but once again the curse of Ely Crusaders had drifted into Essex and their title hopes were dashed!

Our final two league matches of the season were at home to Queens Arms (0-0) and Girton Eagles, against whom we extended our unbeaten league run to nine games by coming from three goals down at half-time to draw 3-3. I didn't score in that particular match, but it was nevertheless a stunning comeback and a sensational contest which mirrored the excitement of our 4-4 draw against the same opponents earlier in the season, when we twice came from behind to again share the spoils. Once more we were a force to be reckoned with in the top flight of Sunday football.

Receiving the Ely Crusaders U-18's Player-of-the-Year trophy from club president Alf Pope.

My uncle Maurice 'Mossy' Murfitt, the provider of my first pair of (ancient) football boots.

My dad Clive Green – loved farming, hated football!

Colchester United Youths in the bar at Pontins in Brean Sands, near Weston-Super-Mare in 1978. I have no idea who the girls are, but I can remember most of the players! Back row L-R: Steve Green, Graham (?) the goalkeeper. Front row L-R: John, Geoff Harrop, Gary Harvey, Russell Cotton, Phil and Tony Evans.

Ely Park Rangers Tour Party on the TuS St Hubert (Kempen, Germany) pitch in 1979. Back row L-R: Bobby Skinner, Alan Mahler, Duncan Scott, Les Cornwell, Steve Green, Rob Gwynn, Ifor Evans, Dave Buckingham, Chris Hughes, Richard Evans, Alun Evans, Linda Evans, Ivor Evans. Front row L-R: Roger Smith, Tony (from Wisbech), Mike Sharpe, Stephen Snell, Mrs Alun Evans.

This photograph of Burble, me, Harry and Rob appeared in the Westdeutsche Zeitung newspaper. Rob and I drove to St Hubert in his Lada (also in picture) and camped in the garden of the Bader family. Someone told the newspaper and suddenly we were famous! Notice the flares...

Me in action during the first 1984/1985 Regional Cup final against South East Region. My National Team colleague Nick Ryan is poised to challenge, but couldn't prevent me scoring twice in a 5-0 success.

The Inland Revenue Eastern Counties team on the eve of the 1986/1987 Regional Cup semi-final against West Midlands Region. We won 2-1 and went on to beat Scotland by the same score in the final to claim the trophy for the third year in a row. Back row L-R: Roland Dean, John Jude, Mark Avery, Ian Alderson, Graham Mann, Dave Pert, Bob McCormick. Front row L-R: Paul Widdowson, Mick Euell, Kevin Cade, (sorry, no idea!), Steve Besford, Steve Green, Alan McDougall.

Soham Town Rangers Reserves in 1987/1988. During my career I consider it to be the best truly 'local' side ever assembled in the Ely/Soham/Littleport area. Back row L-R: Paul Giddens, Steve Mason, Andy Pearson, Graham Eley, Alan Moore, Richard Palmer, David South, our club linesman, Mick Robinson. Front row L-R: Graham Bailey, Kevin Bird, Steve Green, Brian Eley, Gary Chilvers, Gary Goodjohn.

Me clutching the Hoadley Cup as captain of Cambridge Taxes. The 1-0 final win over Yarmouth Taxes in 1990/1991 was our first ever success in the competition, although we went on to retain the trophy the following year.

The Hoadley Cup winning team of 1990/1991. Back row L-R: Richard Savage, Colin Thompson, Nick Wells, Chris Roope, Mark Brown, Richard Miller, Kevin Crouch, Nick Florence, Pete Reece. Front row L-R: Gary Maltby, Nick Howitt, Steve Green, Glynn Carroll, Andy Salter.

CHAPTER ELEVEN: The FA Cups

Ely Crusaders began the 1981/1982 campaign in a similar vein to the previous season, going unbeaten in the first six league and cup outings before I was unavailable for the Sunday League Cup tie at Brooklands United which we surprisingly lost 6-1.

During the opening weeks of the campaign however, we had embarked on our first ever stint in the FA Sunday Challenge Cup. You may not know much about this competition (and indeed, the format may have changed), but for a small self-financing club like Crusaders it was a bloody expensive carry on.

The pitch had to (at least) be roped off to meet the FA requirements for the competition; the team shirts had to be numbered; the home team had to pay half of the away team's travelling expenses; the home team had to pay for the referee and two qualified independent linesmen to officiate at the tie; all participating teams had to meet strict financial and league status requirements in order to enter the competition in the first place. Entering the FA Sunday Cup for the first time was not a decision to be taken lightly by a small club like ours.

In the First Round we drew London-based Carlton United at home, and having won the cup in 1966/1967 and 1972/1973 they had been runners-up in the competition as recently as 1978/1979. Upon arrival at Downham Road in Ely, the Carlton officials were both aloof and dismissive. What had the FA Sunday Cup come to when a club of their stature was forced to travel to the 'sticks' to play a bunch of – what they described as – "country boys"?

The visitors were inevitably hot favourites, and started the tie impressively. Taking an early lead, they were giving us a bit of a footballing lesson but without creating too many clear-cut chances after their early breakthrough. We gradually came back into the game, and towards the end of the first half a throw-in was flicked on at the near post and I was on hand to nod in the equaliser from close range. Carlton suddenly realised they had a match on their hands, and when the second half got underway Crusaders proved more than a match for their illustrious visitors. The tide had undoubtedly turned, and with Carlton never threatening to score again the pressure on them gradually cranked up. It seemed only a matter of time before we took the lead, but when we did score it came from the most unlikely of sources.

Mark Haynes was a product of 'Chic' Cooper's Ely Crusaders youth programme, post-'Midge' Green. He was an unlikely footballer, with bowed legs that made him appear quite ungainly when he ran. But 'Chic' saw something in him and persevered, moulding him into a very useful midfielder who subsequently played league football in Australia. At this point in time he was still an unproven teenager, but he had energy and enthusiasm to spare which served him well in this particular energy-sapping encounter.

Picking up the ball deep inside his own half, he beat one player and moved into opposition territory. Then he beat another opponent. Then another. Finally, there was only the goalkeeper to beat, albeit at the end of a 70-yard run. I was rapidly making my way upfield in the hope of capitalising on Mark's efforts, but I thought the chance had gone when the Carlton goalkeeper made his challenge on the edge of the penalty area. Mark however, just managed to prod the ball upwards and over the 'keeper before he was challenged. Where was it going? Was it square to me? Was it goalwards? Was it wide?

The ball took what seemed like an age to bounce. It looked on target. It bounced again. Was it going to hit the post? It bounced again, only this time nestling in the corner of the net to put us ahead for the first time in the tie.

Carlton United haemorrhaged self-belief to a terminal degree. They were a beaten side. We knew it and they knew it, but the 'piéce-de-resistance' was yet to be delivered.

In the cloyingly wet autumnal conditions, I too was feeling the physical strain. The ball broke to me in the centre-circle just inside Carlton's half, and the best I could do was to prod the ball to the left into the path of Ian Smith. Without breaking stride, Ian timed his effort to absolute perfection. I say 'absolute perfection' without fear of contradiction, because that is precisely what it was – absolute perfection.

He was fully 40 yards from goal when making contact with the ball, and his shot flew. It did not deviate from its path. It flew straight. Unerring. Fast. The goalkeeper was flat-footed. All he could do was watch. The ball slammed into the top right-hand corner of the net, and it was an emphatic reflection of our dominance on the day. As I said earlier, it remains to this day the best, purest strike I have ever seen. Have you ever witnessed perfection? If you have, you would remember. I remember. A cold, grey Sunday morning at Downham Road in Ely, illuminated by the most stunning goal you could imagine. I could only dream of ever striking a ball that well.

So it finished 3-1, and after the game 'Chic' shook hands with the Carlton officials. "Not bad for a bunch of 'country boys', eh?" It was the only time I ever heard him gloat.

At this point in time everything was rosy for me and the team. We were unbeaten in 13 league and cup outings and a trip to newly-promoted Ickleton was next on the agenda. I was in quite unstoppable form, helping myself to a treble as we established a commanding 3-1 lead. I was due to be in action for Ely City at home to Yarmouth Town in the afternoon however, so came off with 10 minutes remaining to conserve my energy. Unfortunately for us Ickleton hit back in my absence to salvage a 3-3 draw.

In the pub afterwards Steve 'Ziggy' Mozejko taught me how to shell prawns (putting him immediately on a culinary coaching par with my former Cambridge City manager Dave 'chicken-etiquette' Worthington), but I couldn't hang about because there was a Town & Country League match against Yarmouth on the horizon. I opened the scoring in that game after Moden's shot had been parried by the goalkeeper, but we had to settle for a 1-1 draw. In fairness though, I was a spent force following the morning game. No wonder I found training such a chore!

I was on target again for Crusaders in the Sunday Challenge Cup 3-2 victory at Bar Hill, and after missing the aforementioned 6-1 cup mauling by Brooklands United I was back in the side for the FA Sunday Cup Second Round tie at Rainham-based Temperance United – and what a dramatic encounter that proved to be.

Rainham's ground was surprisingly ramshackle. I expected something akin to the Southern League standards to which I had briefly become accustomed, but the changing facilities at Rainham made Downham Road look like the Palace of Versailles. We were in determined mood however, and in the early stages Temperance United appeared to be there for the taking. I volleyed Colin McAhren's cross over the line to put us in front, and it looked as if we would be starting the second half with that 1-0 advantage.

The hosts were suddenly awarded a penalty which they converted however, and moments later were awarded another spot-kick which was likewise dispatched, leaving us 2-1 adrift at the interval. We felt no need to panic, but within moments of the second half getting underway Temperance won a third penalty which enabled them to establish an unlikely 3-1 lead. Having been the better side, we found ourselves two goals adrift and staring defeat in the face. Every time the ball was knocked towards our box after that, the home crowd shouted "penalty!" revelling in our apparent misfortune.

Ely Crusaders however, were no quitters. McAhren flicked on a throw-in at the near-post and I controlled the ball on my right thigh before volleying it high into the roof of the net with my left foot to reduce the arrears to a single goal. With pressure mounting again on the home side, substitute Gary Collins then drilled the ball into the bottom left-hand corner of the net to tie the scores at 3-3, which was how it stood at the end of normal time.

Everyone looked exhausted in extra-time and a replay (which would have been a bloody expensive business for us) looked imminent. We were still looking for a winner, but I was dispossessed on the edge of the penalty area and it looked as if our chance had evaporated. Suddenly however, central defender Geoff King appeared on the scene. I will never know to this day what he was doing there, but no matter. He instinctively thrashed the ball into the top right-hand corner to make it 4-3 and send us ecstatically into the last 64 of the competition.

At Ely City meanwhile, our FA Cup star had simultaneously been rising. Having marked my first appearance of the campaign with a double in the 6-2 home league win against Thetford Town, I contributed another brace in the 3-3 First Qualifying Round draw away to local rivals Chatteris Town, where we came back from two goals down to salvage the tie.

Nodding home the 2-1 winner in the home replay and then

participating in the Second Qualifying Round 2-1 victory over Clacton Town, I looked forward to meeting higher-ranked Bedford Town away at the next stage of the competition.

Unfortunately, I was suffering from 'shin-splints' due to the firmness of the pitches at that time of the year, and my condition got gradually worse as the tie progressed. Bedford were no great shakes, but led by virtue of a disputed first half penalty and were hanging on grimly to their advantage. The tie was held up for a few minutes due to a 'pitch-invasion' by the handful of 'Robins' fans led by my cousin Dale (!) but our chance to equalise eventually came with seconds remaining. The ball was laid up to the edge of the area, and Moden stooped to nod it diagonally into my path behind the last defender.

I was clean through, but my shins were hurting like crazy and it was difficult to put one foot in front of the other, let alone run. With the goal at my mercy, I knew what I wanted to do – score with a rising shot over the goalkeeper's left shoulder. But I couldn't manage it. My effort was on target, but it was along the ground and that allowed the 'keeper to parry it wide.

The final whistle sounded and I was devastated. We had lost 1-0 to an inferior side in my opinion, and in the Fourth Qualifying Round our conquerors entertained Wisbech Town – the team we had beaten 7-0 and 3-0 the season before. Bedford comfortably beat the Fenmen in that last qualifying stage, and went on to face Wimbledon in the First Round Proper. Yes, Wimbledon, who went on to win the FA Cup itself in that famous encounter with Liverpool just six seasons later.

In 1981/1982 however, Wimbledon were embarking on only their fifth season in the Football League, having created history six years earlier by becoming the first non-league side in modern history to knock a top-flight team – Burnley – out of the FA Cup before losing 1-0 in a Fourth Round home replay against mighty Leeds United.

I was incapacitated by those 'shin-splints', and went to my local GP to see what could be done about the problem. He told me to get two buckets – one full of very hot water, and one full of ice water – and then plunge my lower legs alternately into one bucket and then the other until I could no longer feel the difference between the respective temperatures.

It was excruciating! Pain ensued that I cannot adequately describe. But it worked!

The only other time I can recall experiencing pain of such intensity was shortly after grabbing a goal for Ely Crusaders against Girton Eagles one Sunday afternoon in the 1982/1983 season. My lower leg was nicked in the process of scoring at the near post, and by the time I got home an 'egg' had formed on my shin where the skin was broken. Well, the pulsing agony I experienced was something else. The following morning I had to go to the surgery and have the haematoma lanced by the doctor. Just thinking about it still makes me wince – and women seem to think that childbirth is painful...

Coincidentally, Girton Eagles were the next opponents at Downham Road in the 1981/1982 season after the jaw-dropping excitement of our victory at Temperance United. Having lost only three of our previous 20 league matches at home, we approached the game against Girton with a merited degree of confidence. Things didn't go our way on this occasion however, and whilst I had no complaints about our 5-1 beating on the day, I did have reason to complain about my first encounter with referee Richard Nichols.

My Ely City team-mate Peter Galenski had already converted two penalty kicks for Girton – both with his left foot (the only foot he possessed) into the bottom right-hand corner – before Nichols saw fit to award the Eagles a third spot-kick. It was consequently the second match in succession in which we had three penalties awarded against us! That must be a record! Galenski duly stepped up and converted the penalty, in exactly the same way as he had dispatched the previous two. However, as with Guy Loveday's shot for Cambridge Hornets some six years earlier, the ball somehow passed through the net.

Was it a goal? Yes, of course it was, but Nichols was the only person in the vicinity who didn't seem aware of the fact. So what did he do? Well, he decided to consult two kids who happened to be standing near the goal-line! They said that they didn't know if the ball had gone in or not, so on the basis of their contribution he disallowed Galenski's penalty hat-trick!

In the season that followed (1982/1983) we were 'lucky' enough to have Nichols on duty for our visit to eventual champions Springbox, and he single-handedly managed to ruin a barnstorming encounter between the two sides.

My dreadful back pass let in Springbox for the opener, but I scored with a thumping header from Ian Smith's corner to redress the balance and it was 2-2 at the break. We trailed again in the second half, but Gary Collins equalised and it looked as if we had secured a well-earned point against the best side in the league. Nichols had other ideas however.

Springbox launched a hopeful ball towards our goal. Full-back Gary Dewey slid into the six-yard box and cleared the danger. What happened next beggared any degree of belief.

Nichols incredibly pointed to the centre-spot, signalling that a goal had been scored. Springbox players looked at each other in astonishment, and we gaped open-mouthed at a decision that defied all logic and common sense. As captain of the team, I asked Nichols to consult our linesman – 'Chic' Cooper – to ask him what had actually happened. 'Chic' confirmed that the ball had not gone anywhere near the goal-line, let alone across it. This made no difference to Nichols however; he ignored everything and maintained that a goal had been scored.

I was dumbfounded. As captain, I didn't know what to do. I considered – very seriously – taking my team off the field of play, but enough time passed to enable me to rationalise that this would have been counter-productive in the longer term. We had lost a match 4-3, but we would have lost infinitely more by undertaking the walk-out I felt was justified.

I hope that anyone reading this will not misunderstand my reaction to this situation. If the ball had gone anywhere near the goal-line, I would have had reason to consider that the referee had made a reasonable judgement in the circumstances. But it was literally nowhere near the line. I can't help thinking that after the Galenski penalty debacle in the previous season, Nichols just simply lost it again.

As mentioned previously, I was a qualified referee and was no cheat. I was playing in defence for Ely Park Rangers one time when a shot came in that brushed my shorts on its way over the bar. The referee awarded a goal-kick, so I respectfully informed him that the ball had brushed my shorts and the correct decision was therefore a corner. He maintained that it was a goal-kick, and I said that this was fine – all I was doing was pointing out that the ball had touched my clothing before going out of play so it should have been a corner. He then threatened to book me for dissent! But he didn't, and as well as never being red-carded I was never once booked for dissent in my entire career. A dozen or so tasty challenges maybe, but no dissent.

Players I greatly respected – Johnny Fretwell, 'Soapy' Edwards and Terry Rider to name but a few – were unable to show such verbal restraint when it came to dealing with referees, but in all honesty there was more chance of me being red-carded for maiming an opponent in a challenge than there was of me being dismissed for dissent! 'Soapy' was particularly notable for his verbal ripostes on the football field, and they were by no means confined to referees. "You fucking trolley!" he would shout, if you passed a ball to him which required slightly more than a canter for him to reach it!

As a qualified referee, I felt on one occasion that it was my duty to respond to (yet) another Robbie Savage radio rant about refereeing decisions, on the basis that he was complaining from a standpoint of ignorance (i.e. as a player who didn't fully understand the *laws of the game*). I therefore screeched the car to a halt one Saturday evening and phoned the 606 programme on Radio Five Live. Savage was about to retire from the professional game at this point in time, and I thought he might be considering a managerial career (heaven help us), in which case he would need to take his coaching badges. Here's how it went...

Dan Walker: Let's speak to Steve. Hi Steve.

Me: Hi there. Yeah, I want to talk about Robbie's referee-bashing. Many ex-players go on to do their coaching badges because they want to be managers, and the reason why the vast majority of them fail is because they don't know the *laws of the game*.

DW: Listen, they do know the *laws of the game*; it's pretty much a waste of time.

Me: What I'm trying to say is that if people like Robbie understood the *laws of the game*, because they would…

Savage: I know the *laws of the game*, Steve. I know the *laws of the game*.

Me: No you don't. And if you think you do…

Savage: Don't tell me what I don't know. I know the *laws of the game*. Don't tell me what I don't know.

Me: No, you don't, and if you think you do, take (interrupted) take…

Savage: Ask me a question then. Ask me a question then.

Me: No, if you think you know the *laws of the game*, take your coaching badge and when you fail, then you ring me back and we can discuss it then.

Savage: What are you on about? Steve, ask me a question. I know the *laws of the game*, ask me a question and I'll prove it to you. Ask me a question.

Me: (Laughs). Just because I ask you one question doesn't prove you know *the laws of the game*.

Savage: Go on, ask me a question. There you go. Don't tell me what I don't (sic) and don't

	know. I know the *laws of the game*.
DW:	I think it's a moot point Steve.
Savage:	Rubbish point Steve.
DW:	Steve, It's a bit of a moot point as to whether he knows the *laws of the game* or not.
Me:	The main point I was trying to get across is why ex-pros fail their coaching badges – it's because they don't know the *laws of the game*, and…
Savage:	Who's failed their coaching badges Steve? Who's failed their coaching badges you know?
Me:	Hundreds and hundreds of ex-professionals.
Savage:	Who?
Me:	Er, well it doesn't matter. See, you just try to put pressure on me for a list of the names. (Whispers) Next time I phone I'll remember to bring a list with me.
Savage:	You have just said to me: 'I don't know the *laws of the game*!' Don't phone up and tell me I don't know the *laws of the game*. I know the *laws of the game*. 'Course I do Dan (Whimpers). I love football. I know the *laws of the game*.
DW:	I know you know the *laws of the game*, and I'm not sure that a lot of players don't

know the *laws of the game*.

Scott Mills – even though he apparently doesn't like football (or dancing, from what I've seen) – used this phone-in discussion as the premise for a 'tongue-in-cheek' competition on the radio a couple of days later. The question he asked was: How many times did they say *'the laws of the game'* during the call-in? (For what it is worth, the answer was 18).

Now I don't listen to Scott Mills and nothing I have seen or heard is likely to alter that. What I did find odd about the *'laws of the game'* competition was his emphasis on the fact that he would be "giving away twenty Scott Mills points for the correct answer". Not 'ten' he emphasised. 'Twenty'. So how much are these Scott Mills points worth? Can you spend them? Can you open an account with the Royal Bank of Scott Mills?

Anyway, after the aforementioned Nichols/Galenski penalty debacle, I was unavailable again as Ely Crusaders suffered yet another 6-1 cup humiliation, this time at Barnwell in the First Round of the Sunday Challenge Cup. All eyes however, were focused on our home FA Sunday Cup clash with mighty Oxford Road Social as we attempted to reach the last 32 of the competition.

Our London-based opponents had a formidable pedigree in the Sunday equivalent of the FA Cup, and I found myself up against towering Cray Wanderers centre-half Tony Pamphlett. I had no idea how good a player he was and Pamphlett had an excellent game, restricting me to three half-chances, but Oxford Road were a very good side and scored once in each half to deservedly progress to the next round.

The immediate reaction to our brave exit from the country's premier Sunday competition was not at all positive, and we were beaten 3-0 at home by Phoenix and 6-0 at Queens Arms to make it three defeats in a row.

Ely City on the other hand, thrived during my shin-splint-induced absence, taking seven points out of a possible 10 in a series of matches involving the likes of Wisbech Town, Gorleston and Sudbury Town. Their form was not so good when I returned to action, but it picked up and I finally grabbed another Saturday goal, this time a header in the 2-0 home win against Stowmarket Town. At this stage of the season, the 'Robins' boasted an impressive unbeaten home record in the Town & Country League, having won five and drawn four of their nine outings at the 'Paradise' ground.

Crusaders meanwhile, were trying to arrest an alarming slide down the Senior Division table on Sundays. I grabbed the only goal in a 1-1 draw at Littlebury, and then repeated the dose as we held them at home two matches later. In between those games I had scored two very early goals at Sawston Keys to put us 2-0 up, but we had then conceded three to go home empty-handed on that occasion.

Our first away league win of the season was an impressive 5-1 victory at Melbourn-based Blades, but my fifth goal in as many games proved fruitless as we went down by the odd-goal in five at home to Ickleton. With our Senior Division status in the balance and with only seven games remaining, I faced a busy weekend with a home clash for Ely City against Colchester United Reserves, a trip to in-form NCI on the Sunday morning and another home match for City in the afternoon, this time against fast-improving Wisbech Town.

I was on fire against Colchester on the Saturday, producing a defence-splitting 40-yard pass for Dave Clarke to open the scoring. I then bamboozled the goalkeeper by flicking the ball past him on his left and then running round the other side before stroking it into an empty net to seal a 2-1 victory.

I had been involved in everything during that game, and in the Crusaders Sunday clash with NCI managed to open the scoring in another crucial 2-1 success. In the afternoon match for City at home to Wisbech I was understandably tired, but came close with a diving header as we extended our unbeaten home record to 12 games with a 0-0 draw.

At that stage of the season City had won 10 and drawn 10 of 26 league outings, but in all honesty the cracks of an ageing squad were beginning to show. This was something that player-manager Lester Newell had seen fit to mention after the goalless encounter with Wisbech, because he knew how lucky we had been to draw against a youthful and emerging Fenland Park outfit. We were "tired" he surmised, and I think this perhaps reflected how he felt in himself at this stage of his career. So much so, that he resigned his position at the end of the season, with the 'Robins' having won only two of their last 17 league games, scoring 16 times and conceding 45.

Oddly enough though, I had been in great form. I scored with headers in the 5-1 home defeat by Clacton Town and the 3-1 midweek defeat at Yarmouth Town, and was on target again when we managed to beat Felixstowe Town 3-1 at home. I then volleyed home spectacularly (past Kevin Murray again) in the 4-1 setback at Haverhill Rovers, and repeated the feat at home to the same opponents (and against the same goalkeeper!) as we lost 2-1.

My final goal of the campaign for Ely City was our consolation in a 5-1 home reverse against Saffron Walden Town, so at that stage of the season – in a struggling side – I had scored six of our 14 goals in 15 matches. I know that most of my fellow players voted for me as player-of-the-year that season, but the Ely City fans also got to vote and had only travelled – by and large – to home fixtures. Consequently it was central defender Pat Hennebry who received the accolade, which was disappointing for me because I felt that in this particular season I had deserved it.

Former Soham Town Rangers striker John Tippett guested for us in the end-of-season 5-2 Soham Charity Cup semi-final defeat at Newmarket Town, scoring both goals prior to his introduction as the new 'Robins' player-manager. This however, was pretty much the 'beginning of the end' for me at Ely City, as Lester Newell handed over the managerial reins.

Crusaders still had to pick up a few points on Sundays in order to avoid relegation, and four from a possible 10 after the NCI win were just sufficient. I finished off the Sunday League season with both goals in a 2-2 draw at Phoenix, giving me 17 in all competitions out of the 41 that Ely Crusaders scored in total. I also made one appearance for Ely Crusaders Reserves, grabbing four goals in the 5-1 home win against Mildenhall Town.

For the Inland Revenue Football Club, we reached the semi-final again and travelled down to face Plymouth Civil Service in Bath. I made a goal for Pete Tilley which gave us a second half lead, but Plymouth recovered to secure a 3-1 victory. In all honesty though, we had all got so rat-arsed the previous evening that I'm surprised we even made it as far as the pitch or the second half!

CHAPTER TWELVE: Eastern Counties

Prior to the 1980/1981 season, the Eastern Counties Inland Revenue representative side did not even exist. Local Revenue offices were finding it increasingly hard to field competitive sides in the Somerset House Cup due to diminishing staff numbers and the increasing prevalence of women in the department. As a result the Eastern Counties team was formed in 1980, with a view to mounting a challenge for the coveted Somerset House Cup. Our first few matches – spread over the first two seasons – just so happened to be against the regions of East London, South London, West London and North London.

The first two matches in 1980/1981 were both friendlies, and even at that early stage I knew I was playing alongside some players who were quite special. John Wilson, with whom I would form productive striking partnerships – both regionally and nationally – over many years, outstanding central defender Steve Besford and tigerish midfielder Kevin Cade were all there at the start of what proved to be something of a footballing dynasty in the Inland Revenue. I grabbed the winner as East London were edged out 3-2 in our opening friendly, and contributed four more as South London were dispatched 6-1 in our second fixture.

The 1981/1982 season saw our first attempt to lift the Somerset House Cup, and we began with a 6-0 demolition of West London in which I scored twice. In the quarter-final we were drawn away to North London, and were brimming with confidence as a result of our impressive start to regional competition. Our hosts had one of the Inland Revenue Great Britain & Northern Ireland players in their team, a lanky Londoner called Gary Stark who played for Erith & Belvedere and was equally effective in the centre of defence or in attack. On this particular day he played up front, and duly produced the best performance I ever saw from him. He won most things in the air, and showed individual brilliance on the ball which stretched our defence to its limits.

We led against the first half run of play, but North London deservedly equalised and it seemed only a matter of time before Stark finished us off. With minutes remaining however, we finally broke into the opposition half and the ball was laid towards me on the edge of the penalty area. At this stage of the tie I could hardly raise one foot in front of the other, because I had been running around fruitlessly as North London camped themselves in our territory.

When the ball reached me, I reacted so slowly that I failed to move my standing left foot. The ball struck it, and suddenly popped up in front of me. With the last ounce of energy remaining, I swung my right foot forward and managed to unleash a dipping volley into the top right-hand corner for what proved to be the 2-1 winner.

It might have looked spectacular, but in truth it owed a great deal to luck. When the ball sits up like that it is far easier to hit with pace, and the only reason it popped up was because I was too knackered to move my foot out of the way!

Mighty Cumbernauld-based Centre 1 were the visitors to Cambridge for the semi-final, and it proved to be a classic encounter. I turned sharply to score one of our first half goals as the lead changed hands more than once, but the teams were locked together at 3-3 at the end of normal time.

Centre 1 went ahead for what looked to be the final time in the 118th minute, but a sensational out-of-the-blue volley from the diminutive Paul Onions tied the scores at 4-4 in the last few seconds of extra-time. So it was down to penalties. Steve Besford struck the bar with our opening spot-kick, but we were foot-perfect thereafter and eventually won the shoot-out 4-3, and it was up to Burton Albion's ground for the final of the Somerset House Cup against Bradford Taxes. The final marked my first ever failure to score in the green and white of Eastern Counties, but my strike partner John Wilson grabbed a hat-trick and we ran out comfortable 3-1 winners on the day.

I was unavailable when Eastern Counties lost for the first time ever in 1982/1983, going down 1-0 at home to Newcastle as we surrendered the Somerset House Cup at the first defence. I later played (but did not score) in a 6-5 friendly win at Manchester Taxes, and in the following season (1983/1984) I was absent, having been struck down with illness as the Eastern Counties lost 2-0 at home to Manchester in the last ever Somerset House Cup. The famous competition was subsequently replaced by the Regional Challenge Cup, with the semi-finals and final being held at Lilleshall Sports Centre.

I had been enjoying the start of the 1984/1985 football season having returned to play for Ely City on Saturdays, but was walking to work in Cambridge one sunny morning when something suddenly 'went' in my foot, about a mile from the office. I couldn't shake it off, and the further I walked the more excruciating the pain became; so much so that by the time I reached the office, I was at a virtual standstill.

Ice treatment did nothing for it, so I was forced to rest for several weeks without having diagnosed the problem. Eventually I came back in a friendly for Eastern Counties which we won 8-1 against North London, and although I scored once the pain was on its way back and I had to leave the field prematurely. I went to see the Cambridge University physiotherapist Roy Carter* at his home in Cottenham, and he proudly boasted that he had never failed to cure anyone. He tried everything, including the attachment of wires to my foot which enabled him to run an electrical current through the affected area. That only made things worse unfortunately, so we decided that I must have suffered a stress fracture. Nothing showed up on the hospital X-rays however, so all I could do was rest.

* Roy Carter used to be the PE Teacher at Witchford Village College. On one occasion he refereed the first half of yet another City of Ely College defeat at their place, but at the interval was replaced by our own PE Teacher Bill Oughton. I saw fit to ask if this was because Roy was tired, and ended up getting a severe slippering for my cheek!

My next comeback attempt from the foot injury was for the Inland Revenue Football Club against the Department of Environment in the Lewis Cup, a match which we eventually won 3-1. In truth I knew that I probably shouldn't have played, but relinquishing your place in the side potentially opened the door for the likes of Manchester-based Dave Booth and Leek Town striker Dave Sutton. I hit the bar twice in that game, but I was badly injured and knew that I had no chance of playing in any subsequent rounds of the 1984/1985 competition.

Dave Sutton played a record 475 games for Leek Town, and his most famous moment came in the 1990/1991 FA Cup when he could be seen on Match of the Day scoring against Football League side Scarborough in a shock 2-0 First Round victory for the non-league side. Leek eventually lost in a Second Round replay against another league side, Chester City. Sutton however, never managed to dislodge me from the Inland Revenue FC starting line-up, even when the team was based and managed in Manchester by John Heapy.

I had recovered from my foot problem sufficiently by the end of the 1984/1985 season to play for Eastern Counties in the closing stages of the first ever Regional Football competition at Lilleshall, scoring once and missing a penalty in the 8-1 semi-final demolition of Northern Ireland. In the final the following day I scored twice more as we proved 5-0 too strong for a South East side which included my National Team colleague Nick Ryan, an athletic full-back who played for Bromley.

The Inland Revenue Football Club had finished runners-up in the 1984/1985 Lewis Cup in my continued absence, so I was pretty much resigned to surrendering my place for the 1985/1986 campaign. Dave Sutton, Dave Booth and several other strikers were unavailable for the First Round clash with HASSRA* (North West) however, so I was fortunate enough to be selected for the tie alongside my Eastern Counties team-mate John Wilson and we travelled North-West to the Civil Service Sports Ground at Timperley.

Health & Safety Regional Association.

Timperley (near Stockport) was one of my favourite hunting grounds. I had played in two friendlies there for the Inland Revenue Football Club, scoring once in each of the 5-3 and 5-0 wins against Manchester Taxes. I had also played in a 6-5 friendly win against the same opponents for Eastern Counties, and in 1983/1984 scored all three goals in a cracking 3-3 draw at the same venue – including a brace of penalties.

I was determined to once again secure my place in the National team, and was in unstoppable form with a well-taken hat-trick as HASSRA (North West) were dispatched 5-1. In the next round – again at Timperley – we were drawn to face Durham National Savings, and although I had suffered strained ankle ligaments shortly beforehand, there was no way I was going to drop out having just regained my place in the Revenue's representative side.

With the tie goalless midway through the first half, a corner in the Durham penalty area was partially cleared and I was lurking on the edge of the box, ready to strike. As I approached the ball for a full-blooded blast through a crowd of players however, I remembered that my ankle was still injured. So at the very last second I decided to side-foot the attempt instead, and it couldn't have worked out better. The ball curled deliciously into the top right-hand corner, giving us the breakthrough we needed.

In truth the goal was maybe lucky because it was only the injury that prevented me from perhaps smashing the ball aimlessly, but it looked great and I added two more goals for a second successive hat-trick as we ran out 3-1 winners.

HASSRA (Midlands) were beaten 2-1 at Sutton Coldfield in the next round, but I remember this tie most for the fact that I missed my train home! I did arrive at the station on time, but inadvertently stood on the wrong side of the track (slightly inebriated) and failed to catch the last train as a result! I ended up sleeping on the floor of a team-mate's room in the Holiday Inn at New Street, Birmingham, and travelled back the following day instead. In the quarter-finals, our interest in the competition was ended by MOD (Main), who grabbed the only goal of the game to win 1-0.

In the Inland Revenue Regional Challenge Cup, Eastern Counties began their defence of the trophy with a difficult tie against the Valuation Office at Ipswich. This was the first time we managed to field the 'dream' forward line of John Jude (Basildon), John Wilson and myself, but it didn't work out as planned. We were lethargic all over the field and soon found ourselves behind, but even when Eastern Counties didn't play well, they were always competitive. I put us back on terms with a spectacular dipping 25-yard left foot volley that went in via the crossbar and the far post, and struck again with a close-range header from John Wilson's cross to make it 3-1. Valuation Office pulled another goal back, but we did not play well on the day and it was a lucky escape for us.

In order to reach Lilleshall again, we had to overcome North London at the Civil Service Sports Ground at Barnes Bridge. Once again we were not at our best, but I played reasonably well and grabbed the only goal of the game with a fine individual effort. Receiving the ball and turning a defender on the halfway line, I made my way to the left side of the penalty area before cutting back on my right foot and curling a drive just inside the far post past goalkeeper Loudon Muir.

In the semi-final at Lilleshall we faced Manchester Taxes, who really fancied their chances of beating us. They began well, and before we knew it we were two goals down. Manchester then thought they had scored a third goal on the stroke of half-time, but Steve Besford managed to slide back into the six-yard box and hook the ball clear of danger.

The second half was a different story altogether, as Eastern Counties at last rediscovered their best form. I didn't score myself, but John Wilson helped himself to a hat-trick as we eventually ran out 4-2 winners and could have won by a lot more in the end. Manchester were distraught, and in the evening we happened to find ourselves occupying seats in the same Indian restaurant as our vanquished opponents. Manchester striker Steve Fellows, who I always felt was too greedy on the ball and never managed to establish himself as a regular fixture in the Inland Revenue Football Club, took this opportunity to describe the Eastern Counties team as 'rubbish' within earshot of our huge Scottish central defender Dave Pert.

Well, 'Perty' – a member of the first ever Inland Revenue Football Club side to win the Lewis Cup back in

1977/1978 – went absolutely mad. The rest of the Eastern Counties players had to physically restrain him from tearing Steve Fellows apart, limb by limb. It's one thing to say that a team is rubbish when you have beaten them soundly, but when your opponents have come from two goals down to absolutely thrash you it's perhaps best to keep your mouth shut. Fortunately for Steve Fellows, we managed to keep 'Perty' from beating him to a pulp. Unfortunately for Steve Fellows, his mouth had been more offensive than his boots.

In the final – against South-East Region for the second year in a row – we were again rather subdued, possibly as a result of the excessive drinking after our victory against Manchester. We led through Steve Besford's header, but our opponents equalised and forced extra-time. This produced no resolution, so we embarked on a penalty shoot-out to decide the winners. I took the third penalty as usual (and scored), leaving 'Perty' to gleefully blast home the decisive penalty and spark off another round of wild Eastern Counties celebrations.

In 1986/1987 we began our defence with a 7-0 demolition of West London, and I contributed four goals to that win before adding the winner in a 2-1 war of attrition against East London when I was man-marked throughout. So we were back at Lilleshall again, and despite having won the Regional Challenge Cup twice in a row we were perhaps the least fancied of the four teams that arrived there.

Our semi-final opponents West Midlands were strongly tipped to beat us, and in a one-sided first half they certainly looked the part. We improved after the break however, and a move involving myself and John Jude on the halfway line gave him the chance to cross for Kevin Cade to open the scoring. Little Kevin didn't score many goals with his feet, so what made this one special was that he scored it with his head! Jude then rounded the goalkeeper to make it 2-0, and although West Midlands pulled one back towards the finish we were through to the final to face hot favourites Scotland.

Scot 'Perty' was understandably very familiar with the Scottish lads, so on the night before the final they did their best to get him absolutely bladdered. They pretty much succeeded, and the rest of us were not far behind him so the following morning we woke up with pounding heads, and 'Perty' was a virtual zombie. Some might say that this was how he behaved most of the time, but on this particular occasion he was in one hell of a state.

As the final began, I remember one of the Scotland players telling his team-mates to target the centre of our defence, and in particular our still inebriated central defender. "Come on lads," he said. "He's breathing out of his arse!" And so he was, but Scotland reckoned without Dave's minder, Steve Besford. Whatever Dave missed, 'Bessie' didn't, and Scotland were unable to make the breakthrough they expected.

At the other end, I was getting a hard time from the Scottish defenders, who had been warned that I was the danger-man following my influential performance in the semi-final. We had a throw-in on our left wing, and I was being jostled from behind. So when the ball was delivered, I threw my head back slightly into the face of my marker because he was so close. The referee stopped the game and spoke to both of us, and the Scottish players urged their team-mate to calm down before he did something stupid. The ball was delivered a second time, and as I turned towards goal just inside the area my marker almost inevitably did something stupid - he hacked me down to concede a penalty.

I gleefully dispatched the spot-kick into the top right-hand corner, and although Scotland equalised before half-time their pre-match confidence had been drained by our tenacity. In the second half we opened up their defence with alarming regularity, and with 15 minutes remaining John Jude sped behind their back-line and squared the ball for me to tap home the 2-1 winner into an empty net.

In my experience Scots are often ungracious losers, and on this occasion – when they expected to win handsomely with their comparative array of stars – they took their defeat particularly badly. So much so that their runners-up medals flew across the dressing room, never to be recovered – except by the cleaners.

For the Inland Revenue Football Club, the 1986/1987 season marked the beginning of my striking partnership with the bulldozing Paul Patey. In some ways my goalscoring prowess was eclipsed however, because I was predominantly the provider in our relationship. DHSS London North were dispatched 8-4, ATESA were thrashed 9-0, and Agricola were humbled 7-0, but I only contributed one of those 24 goals. I was not concerned by this, because the manager – Billy McLaren – knew exactly what my attributes were and if I wasn't scoring it meant that I was helping someone else to find the net.

I was missing for the 1-1 home draw with HASSRA (North West), but returned for the replay held in Toxteth, Liverpool. Kevin Cade and I travelled up on the day of the match, and when we arrived it was clear that our team-mates – all of whom had stayed overnight – were rather worse for wear. HASSRA scored the only goal of the first half, and McLaren – never one to suffer fools lightly – was less than pleased by his team's performance. At the interval, winger Colin Ross was the first of our players to feel McLaren's Scottish ire.

"Colin," he fumed. "You've been standing a yard from the touchline for the whole of the first half, so in the second half you can do the same – but on the other side of the touchline." Colin Ross never played for the Inland Revenue Football Club again. Things didn't improve much in the second period, but Kevin and I fought against the odds and I was presented with the most fortunate of equalisers.

Standing on the edge of the penalty area after a failed attack, one of the HASSRA defenders inexplicably decided to pass the ball back to his goalkeeper from midway inside his own half. The ball flew directly to my feet, and after side-stepping the advancing 'keeper I steered the ball into an empty net to make it 1-1.

That proved to be a false dawn however, and HASSRA deservedly scored again to claim a 2-1 victory. Billy McLaren was not best pleased. In the dressing room afterwards, he singled out every player for criticism – apart that is, from Kevin and myself, who seemed to be more embarrassed by the fact that McLaren had lambasted everyone apart from us!

For one reason or another, the Eastern Counties team was breaking up at this time, and when the 1987/1988 campaign got underway we had no expectations of retaining our Regional Challenge Cup title for a fourth successive year. I scored as we beat London Region 4-1 in the opening round of the competition, but when we travelled to Manchester in the next stage of the competition I looked around me and feared the worst. Dave Pert was no longer there, and neither was Steve Besford. Manchester on the other hand were still extremely strong, and when they led 3-0 at the interval a severe hammering looked on the cards.

In seven seasons with Eastern Counties I had yet to personally experience defeat, and despite the odds being stacked against us on this occasion I was not about to give that record up lightly. When the second half got underway, I put myself about and my efforts were rewarded with a diving header at the near post which reduced the arrears to 3-1. Manchester knew what I was capable of, and for a moment seemed threatened by my presence as I nearly scored a second. I was denied on the goal-line however, and there were no further goals. I had lost in the colours of Eastern Counties for the first time, and I had tasted defeat against Manchester Taxes for the first time. It marked the end of an era.

For the Inland Revenue Football Club, we were again undone at the semi-final stage of the Lewis Cup. I had scored once in the 5-0 win against HASSRA (London South), and three times in the 13-1 win over Pisces, but failed to hit the target in the 4-2 win over Customs & Excise and again fired blanks as Plymouth Civil Service beat us 3-0 in the last four. In the five seasons that followed however, we were to create Inland Revenue Football Club history.

CHAPTER THIRTEEN: Paradise Lost

The departure of Ely City player-manager Lester Newell at the end of the 1981/1982 Town & Country League season resulted in the appointment of a new player-manager in 1982/1983 – schoolteacher John Tippett.

I think it is fair to say that Tippett – a tall striker who was the spitting image of the Yorkshire Ripper – was no footballing 'workhorse', although he certainly knew where the goal was. This was because he spent most of every match hanging around next to it. Now that's all very well when your opponents are inferior, but when your own team is struggling you need everyone to work as hard as possible and that simply wasn't one of Tippett's attributes. As far as John was concerned, the six-yard box was the pitch. He had little involvement in what went on in other areas, and – in my opinion – little understanding of what needed to happen to facilitate those close-range opportunities on which he thrived.

His laid-back approach to football mechanics was apparent during the pre-season period, which could only loosely be described as 'training'. It was a bad joke waiting to be told, and which would have repercussions for years to come at Ely City.

After playing in a 1-1 evening draw at Royston in which Colin McAhren scored an individual wonder-goal, I went on a tour of Europe with my friends whilst City played out the remainder of their friendlies. A 1-0 defeat at Great Shelford, a 2-2 draw with Cambridge City and an 8-3 defeat of Anglian Combination side Lakenheath gave no real indication that the wheel nuts were as loose as the change in a trampolinist's pocket.

Only myself, Peter Galenski, Bob Lyon, Richard Goodjohn and Pat Hennebry remained from the 1981/1982 squad, but John 'Soapy' Edwards – who had signed for Soham Town Rangers in the close season – changed his mind and decided to re-sign for Ely. Big mistake.

So the 1982/1983 era of John Tippett got underway. He proved himself a true poacher over the years with the likes of Soham Town Rangers, Newmarket Town and Saffron Walden Town, but with the work-rate of a tortoise in the Sahara he was never going to succeed in a poor side; which is exactly what he had proceeded to assemble. Don't get me wrong, most of the players he introduced were really nice guys. Unfortunately however, the likes of Dale Burch, Martin Churchley and Mick Sheehan were simply not good enough to make an impact at this level. They were very good County League players, but they did not have the attributes of players like Pat Hennebry, Johnny Fretwell or Trevor Moden.

An opening day 2-0 loss at March Town United was widely condemned as a 'negative performance,' and that was followed by a 1-0 midweek defeat at Histon. The closest we came to scoring in that game was when I hit the bar with an attempted cross, and already – in the absence of close-season Soham Town Rangers acquisition Moden – questions were being asked as to where the goals would be coming from.

Colin McAhren's shock opener in the 6-1 Eastern Counties League Cup defeat at Haverhill did nothing to allay those concerns, but the club's worries were temporarily shelved when goals in the opening 20 minutes from Goodjohn and Galenski secured a 2-1 league victory at home to Histon. After the concession of those two early goals however, the Cambridge side once again dominated possession and were unlucky to lose.

My solitary consolation goal in the 4-1 defeat at Clacton Town was no consolation because they were considered to be one of the league's weakest teams (even though Ely had won at Old Road only once in 18 league visits), and that was followed by a 2-0 setback at the hands of Saffron Walden, who should have won by a much bigger margin. We only managed two goal attempts in that game, the first of which was in the 67th minute!

At Ely Crusaders meanwhile, we had opened our Sunday League campaign with a useful 2-2 draw at Littlebury, courtesy of goals from Marcus Humphry and Steve Atkin. This was followed by a 4-2 home defeat in the first ever meeting with our Ely rivals BSC, in which goals from myself and debutant Alan Draper failed to repair the damage of a dubious penalty award when the sides were locked together at 1-1 on the hour.

On Saturdays things continued to go from bad to worse for Ely City, who ended the week with only pointless Thetford Town beneath them in the table. 'Soapy' Edwards was the consolation scorer in a 5-1 mauling at Chatteris Town, and I was side-lined with injury as Saffron Walden handed us a 7-0 beating in the return fixture at Catons Lane. An improved performance followed in the First Qualifying Round of the FA Cup at home to fellow strugglers Lowestoft Town, but it still ended in a 3-1 defeat.

Laughably, City at this stage launched a campaign asking supporters to sponsor the club for each goal scored, stating that over the past six seasons the average number was 66. On the evidence of this particular season's efforts at that point in time, any fan that signed up was unlikely to find themselves in financial difficulties as a result!

Back on Sundays I was amongst the scorers as Crusaders claimed their first league victory of the season 4-1 at home to NCI, and the following Saturday at Ely City we secured our first away point of the campaign with a mind-numbing 0-0 draw at Newmarket Town. By this time however, we had already sunk to the bottom of the Eastern Counties League table.

A 1-0 defeat at Bury Town left any 'cash for goals' supporters with their bank balances still intact, whilst the following day saw Ely Crusaders contest an epic FA Sunday Cup tie at the Ravenhill Recreation Ground against Brereton Town – a team based around Stafford Rangers players and arguably the best Sunday League side in the Midlands at that time. A blood-curdling encounter saw us valiantly take the lead 20 minutes from the end of normal time courtesy of a Marcus Humphry header, but heroic goalkeeper Roger Smith was finally beaten in the 87th minute as Brereton made it 1-1.

We had given everything we had during normal time, and the hosts eventually ran out 5-1 winners with four unanswered goals in the extra period. After extensive drinking in the clubhouse afterwards, we travelled back on the coach and passed the bin round for some communal vomiting. I took my turn to throw up and ejected my denture at the same time, but quickly recovered it from the sick-filled bin and immediately put it back into my mouth!

Ely City were also in cup action as they travelled to Arlesey for a midweek FA Vase clash, where three home goals in the first 15 minutes rendered 'Soapy' Edwards' 55th minute goal redundant. Things were still improving for Crusaders on Sundays however, and after four successive 2-2 draws with Phoenix we finally edged them out as I struck twice – with a fierce drive and a glancing header – in a 3-2 victory away from home.

'Soapy' scored another consolation goal the following Saturday as Ely City crashed 4-1 at home to Tiptree United, and if we weren't in enough trouble already the departure of central defender Pat Hennebry to Cambridge City left us in even direr straits.

'Player-manager' Tippett grabbed his first goal of the season after coming on as 75th minute substitute in the 5-2 defeat at Sudbury Town, after I had spectacularly volleyed home only my second City goal of the campaign to reduce the home side's 5-0 advantage. It was at this point in time – in late October 1982 – that Tippett parted company with the club 'by mutual agreement'. His final match 'in charge' was to be the derby clash with Soham Town Rangers, who after going unbeaten in their first seven league games were now experiencing problems of their own following the departure of Trevor Moden and Gary Grogan to Cambridge City. They still beat us however, and although we were not flattered by the 3-0 scoreline it was galling that our former player-manager Lester Newell was amongst the goalscorers, alongside two-goal Ray Brown who likewise had been a City player the previous season.

Thirty-five year-old midfielder Ted Robbins was subsequently revealed as the new player-manager for the 'Robins'. Meanwhile a miserable weekend of football was concluded as Crusaders lost 2-1 at Histon United in the Sunday Challenge Cup, despite my late goal. The same scoreline saw us lose at home to bogey side Queens Arms in the league the following week, when 'keeper Roger Smith saved his fourth penalty out of five but to no avail.

Robbins' first match in charge at City heralded a 2-0 home win over fellow strugglers Thetford Town, but we were still bottom of the table on goal difference and it was almost inevitably a false dawn. The following Saturday we lost 4-3 at Soham in the Cambs Invitation Cup, having drawn level three times before conceding the winner in extra-time. I had thumped in a header for my third City goal of the season to make it 2-2 in the second half, which proved to be the only goal I ever scored against Rangers.

Things soon returned to normal at City however, as four first half goals went unanswered in the league defeat at

Tiptree. I scored for Crusaders from the penalty spot on the Sunday however, contributing to a 4-1 League Cup Second Round success at Soham-based rivals Angle Rangers. Another goal followed seven days later as we won 3-2 at Girton Eagles in the Senior Division, but as mentioned previously I was cut on the shin by the goalkeeper as I swivelled to fire home the winner and this resulted in an infected haematoma which had to be lanced by my GP the following day.

There had been another goalless game for Ely City the previous day in the 3-0 loss at Stowmarket Town, but three goals went in at home to Wisbech Town the following Saturday, a game I missed because of my lacerated shin. Unfortunately the visitors overturned a 3-1 interval deficit to win by the odd goal in seven after player-manager Robbins was caught in possession in the 90th minute. I was also absent for the Crusaders 3-0 Sunday League Cup win at TRC Teversham, City's subsequent 4-0 mauling at Brantham and the 3-3 home draw with fellow strugglers Clacton Town.

The New Year (1983) began for Ely City with an unlucky 1-0 loss at Braintree, followed by a 2-0 home defeat at the hands of Bury Town which Robbins described as "an absolute shambles." He went on to say that he "had a few cheats" in the side that Saturday, but there was no chance that I was one of them because I was still recovering from injury. City were now back at the foot of the table, courtesy of Thetford's 2-0 win at Haverhill. I had returned to Sunday action however, and struck twice against Senior Division bottom club NCI to give Crusaders a 2-0 lead with 10 minutes remaining, only for the visitors to salvage an unlikely point with two goals of their own. The following Sunday I was on target again on the stroke of half-time, equalising with a shot from the tightest of angles to earn a useful 1-1 draw at Sawston Keys.

City had no game the following Saturday, and on the Sunday Crusaders entertained bitter rivals Littlebury in the quarter-finals of the League Cup. The visitors were lying second in the Senior Division table at the time, and a typically robust first half finished goalless. Gary Chilvers fired us ahead three minutes into the second period however, and I was then upended in the box for a penalty which Gary Dewey dispatched to make it 2-0.

I then scored one of the more fortunate goals of my career. A long clearance from goalkeeper Roger Smith allowed me to get behind the Littlebury defence, and although my first effort was blocked the ball rebounded into my face and ballooned back into the net. Ian Smith added number four with a typically majestic effort, and I wrapped up a 5-0 win from close range after the visiting goalkeeper had failed to hold a Chilvers free-kick. This was undoubtedly one of the best Sunday performances I was ever involved in (and probably the heaviest defeat ever suffered by Littlebury), earning us a semi-final clash with Queens Arms.

The following weekend saw Ely City reach the midway point in their Town & Country League programme with a 2-0 home defeat by March, leaving us rooted to the bottom of the table with just six points. The following day came the Richard Nichols refereeing debacle at Springbox which I have already described in *Chapter Eleven: The FA Cups.*

Back in the Town & Country League, City were still looking for their first goal of 1983, as Lowestoft's 5-0 win at the Paradise Ground was followed by a 1-0 win for visiting Yarmouth. The following Saturday former player-manager John Tippett returned to the Paradise with Newmarket Town, and – unfortunately for us – scored twice in a 5-0 win for the 'Jockeys'. Chatteris then came to our patch and won 4-0, although I did have some chances to score in that one. That was followed by a 3-0 defeat at

Lowestoft – our eighth match in succession without a goal.

Things were not looking quite so rosy on Sundays either, and a 4-2 home defeat by Selser meant that we were being dragged into a relegation dogfight. Goals from Ian Smith and myself had reduced the deficit to 3-2 at one stage, but a late penalty award enabled the visitors to put the match beyond recall.

Another defeat materialised for Ely City the following Saturday, as former 'Robin' Ray Brown struck the only goal of the game in the loss at Soham Town Rangers. We had now played 818 minutes without scoring, and the Ely Standard Sports Editor Brian Knighton suggested the following in his report: *'Perhaps the use of Steve Green, a proven goal-getter, as an out-and-out striker rather than a midfield man, might be advisable.'* I couldn't have agreed more.

On the Sunday Crusaders faced Littlebury at home again, this time in the league. It was 1-1 at half-time, but in the dying minutes of the second period man-of-the-match Geoff King launched a long, hopeful pass towards me down the middle. I outpaced the covering defender Bob Starr, but was brought down in the process of getting away from him. The referee perhaps deemed the tackle a fair one or played a shrewd advantage, but either way I hauled myself off the floor and chipped the advancing goalkeeper from long range to secure a crucial 2-1 win.

Ely City were out of luck again as a late goal cost them their first point of 1983 in a 1-0 defeat at Felixstowe. Things were starting to look up on Sundays though, as Crusaders reached the League Cup Final for the first time in their history with a 1-0 victory over Queens Arms at Stretham. I was initially credited with the decisive goal, but when interviewed afterwards by a Cambridge Evening News journalist I confessed that the ball had in fact been deflected in off unsighted defender John Lane. The subsequent headline *'Finalist Green comes clean'* did little to harm my sporting integrity!

I seem to recall suffering from shin-splints (again) at this time, because I was unavailable for three games the following weekend, including Ely Crusaders' 2-2 home draw with in-form Girton Eagles. On the Saturday Ely City had lost 3-0 at home to Colchester United Reserves, but on the Sunday Mick Sheehan struck the team's first goal in 1000 minutes to provide them with an early lead against title-chasing Gorleston. The visitors eventually ran out 6-1 winners of that game, but at least it was a breakthrough of sorts! It proved to be a trickle rather than a flood however, and two late goals in the next fixture at home to Braintree went unanswered by us before the return clash with Felixstowe ended in a 1-0 defeat.

On Sundays Crusaders were still in relegation trouble, and a 4-1 home defeat by already-crowned champions Springbox compounded that. I scored a cheeky goal by slipping the ball to one side of the goalkeeper, and running around the other side before slotting home a first-time shot, but it was scant consolation in the circumstances.

Back at Ely City there was a Good Friday 3-0 home defeat awaiting us at the hands of Brantham, and an identical result the following day at home to Haverhill when I limped off with ankle ligament damage in the 12th minute. The Ely Standard responded to this latest set of results by proclaiming that we were 'record-breakers', and that it was certain to be the club's worst season in their 23-year Eastern Counties League tenure.

- Already a long way adrift at the bottom of the table, we were condemned to finish there for the third time (the last time having been 18 seasons earlier).

- Barring a miracle, we were certain to finish with the least points, most defeats, least goals scored and most goals conceded.

- We had suffered the most consecutive defeats ever (standing at 16 at the time of the article).

- We had suffered the most games without scoring, both overall and consecutively.

(As if those statistics were not embarrassing enough, City next turned up with only nine men at Colchester United Reserves, going down 7-1!)

Ely City could not be relegated from the Town & Country League, but the spectre of relegation still loomed over Ely Crusaders. We were locked on 12 points with third-from-bottom local rivals BSC, but their final match of the season was at home to us, whilst we still had five games remaining. BSC won the match 2-1 to give themselves a chance of avoiding the drop, leaving us needing a minimum of three points from our last four games to overhaul them. First of all however, there was the Sunday League Cup Final against Newmarket Valley to contend with, that match having already been described fully in *Chapter Two: The Start of the 'Crusades.'*

Defeats for Ely City at Haverhill (3-0), at Thetford (2-1) and at home to Sudbury (0-6) made it 20 league defeats in a row, a run which mercifully came to an end when Stowmarket were held 2-2 at the Paradise.

Still frustrated by my serious ankle injury, I had to stand and watch as Ely Crusaders nose-dived to what I could only describe in my match report as a 'pitiful' 5-1 home defeat against Phoenix, a result which enabled them to leapfrog us and leave us in the bottom two. My report also contained the following comments, which I believe are self-explanatory:

'All most players have to do is turn up with their boots and play, invariably unaware of the constant hard work and effort behind the scenes in order to raise funds to provide the amenity of football. There are also the others doing unrewarded toil in other aspects of a football club. Is it too much to ask for the players to put in 100% effort for 90 minutes on a Sunday to make it worthwhile for those people?'

The following Sunday's clash with Selser was a marked improvement, a match in which I played when I probably shouldn't have done. Ian Smith's corner was turned into the Selser net to earn us a 1-1 draw – the first time we had managed to avoid defeat in the corresponding away fixture against that team. The result left us needing two points from as many games to avoid the drop, or one point and a defeat by two goals or less. As it turned out, we only needed the first of those games at home to Sawston Keys. We trailed 2-1 in the second half, but goals from Gary Collins and Marcus Humphry earned us a crucial 3-2 win.

One of the remarkable things about that game involved our central defender Geoff King. Early in the second half he nodded the ball clear, but an onrushing Sawston forward butted him squarely on the temple and with considerable force, rendering him virtually unconscious and causing him to fit. The game was held up for 20 minutes awaiting an ambulance, and in the meantime Ely Park Rangers' Bryan Saddington – a local fireman – was substituted on the adjoining pitch to enable him to offer first aid assistance to our stricken defender!

Ely City ended their catastrophic Town & Country League campaign by suffering an 8-0 defeat at Yarmouth – their heaviest defeat of the season. It took their goals conceded record up to 129 in just 42 league matches. Crusaders also wound the season up with a heavy defeat – 6-1 at Queens Arms – but we had at least preserved our Senior Division status for another season, finishing fourth from bottom. One less point would have seen us finish in the bottom two, but as it turned out Phoenix – probably the most successful Cambridgeshire Sunday League team in history at the time – were the side to go down.

CHAPTER FOURTEEN: Fever Pitch

Following the debacle of Ely City's 1982/1983 campaign, I signed for Town & Country League rivals Bury Town in the summer of 1983. Their player-manager Martin Spore worked at the Cambridge Valuation Office, and having seen me play in an office game he was impressed enough to ask me along.

Training went well and I was perhaps the fittest I had been since my days at Kings Lynn, and although our pre-season matches did not go particularly well, Spore was gelling together a young squad of considerable potential.

Trevor Sadd (Lowestoft Town) and Derek Richardson (Haverhill Rovers) were recruited in midfield, and Russell Osman's brother Murray excelled at full-back alongside experienced former Ipswich Town defender Les Tibbott. Up front alongside me was the volatile and enigmatic Chris Hughes, who was by no means a typical target man in the mould of someone like Trevor Moden. We nevertheless began to form a decent-looking partnership and in our first league fixture at Chatteris Town managed to put the 'Lilywhites' defence to the sword.

Hughes helped himself to a hat-trick, and I wrapped up a 5-1 win by firing Richardson's pass inside the goalkeeper's right-hand upright for a pleasing debut goal.

We next earned a hard-fought 1-1 draw at Histon, but I was then missing for a fortnight because – prior to signing for Bury – I had already booked a holiday with my mates. The holidays I enjoyed with my friends – Clint, Sean, Jeff, Rob and Kev amongst them – were no ordinary affairs. We did not act like idiots in Ibiza, get trashed in Tenerife, make mugs of ourselves in Malia or absorb as much alcohol as we could in Albufeira. No, we explored the countries of Central and Eastern Europe in a sky-blue tin can otherwise known as a mini-bus, camping outdoors most of the time.

The sky-blue tin can in question was the City of Ely College bus, which was normally used to transport kids from the main building in Downham Road to Bedford House in the city centre, or sometimes took teams to other schools for sporting fixtures. It was driven by Alun Evans, who was the eldest son of Ivor Evans, the co-founder, manager, chairman and ultimately life president of Ely Park Rangers FC.

Alun – a stick-thin, long-haired, bearded throwback to the flower-power days of the 1960s – played for Ely Park Rangers for many years, but was not a gifted footballer. Peter Turnbull – another stalwart of the Ely Park Rangers set-up – once described Alun as the only footballer he had ever seen who could allow the ball to pass through his stomach! Peter was hilarious. I remember going with him into a pub in London once with a group of players, and when he asked the barman for a drink, he was asked if he wanted it in a glass (as opposed to a mug). Peter replied "No thanks, I'll have it in a paper bag."

So Ivor organised these holidays travelling around Europe, and Alun drove the bus for us. We stayed in hotels occasionally, but generally speaking slept in tents on official camp sites. We visited many places including Bruges, Strasbourg, Trier, Heidelberg (twinned with Cambridge), Freiburg, Bonn, Cologne, Salzburg, Assmannshausen, Rudesheim, Luxembourg, Lucerne, Como, Fuschl-am-See, St Wolfgang, St Gilgen, Hallstadt, Vienna, Verona, Venice, Vaduz and even Porec, in what was then Yugoslavia (now Croatia).

I was swimming in the sea one day at Porec when I looked to my right and saw a human turd float past me. In hindsight, I think it is safe to say that the water was polluted, and not the healthiest environment for a holiday-maker. On the way back from Porec I started to feel decidedly unwell. Our next stop was Rudesheim on the River Rhine, and luckily we were staying in a hotel rather than camping out that evening.

If you have ever been to Rudesheim, you will be aware of the so-called *Street of a Thousand Wine Bars*. There are not quite that many bars of course, but certainly enough to get you very inebriated in a short space of time and prancing around like an idiot to renditions of the *Birdy Song* and other German forms of 'Terpsichorean Muse'. I had been there once before and knew what an absolutely fantastic evening it would be, so the fact that my mates partied all night whilst I was laid up in bed shows just how ill I actually was. The doctor was called to examine my extremely sore throat, but there was nothing he could do and as we were already on the journey home the best thing I could do was rest for the time being.

When we got back home I was still unwell and didn't know what was wrong with me. Martin Spore rang upon my return and asked me if I could be substitute for the Tuesday night game at Saffron Walden Town, and I accepted, thinking that this would enable me to get back into the squad and believing that I would feel much better by the time Saturday came around. With eight minutes remaining at Saffron Walden the manager asked me to go on, and when I ran on to the pitch I simply crumpled to the ground. I now realised that there was something very seriously wrong with me.

I went to the doctor the following day, and he informed me that glandular fever was the most likely diagnosis. This was confirmed by a blood test, at which point the doctor advised me of the unpredictable nature of the disease. Some people recover in a few weeks he said, but others could take years or anything in between. I never normally had time off sick, but on this occasion was absent from work for about six weeks. The only thing I can say about my personal experience of glandular fever is that it is utterly debilitating, and although I returned to work after six weeks it was more like six months before I fully recovered.

When I started playing Saturday football again, it was for Adrian Davies' Bury Town Reserves side in the Suffolk & Essex Border League. Still quite weak as a result of the illness I had suffered, I struggled to regain both my form and my fitness in the weeks that followed. My team-mates, all of whom hailed from Suffolk were – predictably in the circumstances – quite sceptical about my footballing ability, because unless you have had glandular fever yourself the chances are that you will have no idea about the impact it can have, both physically and mentally.

I finally made a breakthrough in the match at Clacton Town Reserves. We were trailing 1-0 with seconds remaining when a cross was knocked into the Clacton penalty area, and I made a strong challenge on the goalkeeper. The ball popped up between us, and as we both fell to the ground I managed to half-volley it into the roof of the net to earn us an unlikely point.

By the end of the 1983/1984 campaign I had helped myself to seven league goals and also earned a brief recall to the first team, but perhaps my best performance was in the A V Lee Services Memorial Cup. This was a trophy contested by the previous season's Suffolk & Essex Border League champions (Earls Colne) and the previous season's League Cup winners – Bury Town Reserves. The midweek tie was held at Sudbury Town's ground, and Earls Colne were hot favourites to beat us. I managed to unsettle their defence with an aggressive performance however, and we eventually ran out 2-1 winners.

At the end of the season I was voted runner-up player-of-the-year for the Reserves, and this was a welcome reward for the hard work I had put in on the field since my illness, despite not training with the team due to the travel costs involved. I recall that we drew several league games 2-2 – at home to Sudbury Wanderers, and away at Haverhill Rovers and at Rowhedge. I will always remember playing at Rowhedge in Essex, but only because it is apparently one of just two places in Britain where someone is known to have been killed by an earthquake.

Bury Town Reserves manager Adrian Davies and his wife Corinne were very good to me, and I stayed at their house on several occasions after matches. They moved away at the end of the season however, and this – along with the considerable cost of travelling to and from Bury St Edmunds – prompted my simultaneous departure from the club. I will however, always be grateful to Ady, Corinne and the Reserve team players for accepting me into their 'family' and helping me to recover both my health and my confidence.

For Ely Crusaders I missed the opening day of the 1983/1984 season – a 1-0 defeat at home to the champions Springbox – and was also absent for the 2-1 Challenge Cup defeat at Barwell Sports. Our next match at the end of September 1983 was at home to Littlebury, who in their previous eight encounters with us had managed just three draws and no wins. I laid on close-range goals for Gary Collins and Marcus Humphry to put us 2-0 ahead, but we were pegged back to 2-2 and it looked as if the spoils would be shared. In the last minute however, Richard Goodjohn took a free-kick on the right and I escaped my marker to score with a pinpoint header from 15 yards. So for the third time in four seasons, this Senior Division fixture had been decided by a last minute goal in favour of Crusaders, and on each occasion that winner had been scored by me! Littlebury absolutely detested me, and their manager at the time – Martin Marriott – saw fit to kick a hole in the changing room door!

Crusaders were then at their best to defeat Queens Arms 4-2, and we progressed to the Third Round of the League Cup by winning 2-1 at Barnwell. The hosts led early on, but I levelled things with a towering header from Goodjohn's cross and was then pushed for the penalty which Gary Dewey converted for the winner.

In the meantime – on 3 November 1983 to be precise – my former team Ely City gained their first point of the 1983/1984 season courtesy of a 2-2 draw at home to Stowmarket, and were only denied their first win in 40 games by a late penalty.

Crusaders were drawn at home to Garrington Sunday in the Second Round of the FA Sunday Cup, and we got off to the worst possible start. Only 30 seconds had elapsed when goalkeeper Roger Smith was seriously injured in a collision which saw the visitors take the lead. We got back on terms and I put us 2-1 ahead from the penalty spot, but a stoppage time winner in the second half eventually put us out of the competition. My goal in the tie meant that I ultimately had a record of scoring precisely four goals in each FA competition – the FA Youth Cup, the FA Cup and the FA Sunday Cup!

I scored with a powerful far post header to clinch a 3-2 Senior Division win at Exning United the following week, but our good start to the league season was dismembered by a Sawston Keys side claiming their first victory of the campaign. We trailed 5-0 when I pulled a goal back with a diving header from 15 yards, but as I said in the match report 'the final five minutes summed up Ely's day.' I tore a hamstring, Alan Draper volleyed into his own net and the visitors added a seventh goal for good measure.

A Steve Green-less Crusaders struggled through to the next round of the Sunday League Cup with a 2-1 home victory against lower league Bar Hill, whilst at Ely City player-manager Ted Robbins finally resigned due to 'personal problems'. I don't know if that was the case or not; certainly 44 league games without victory and the humiliation of another hat-trick from former incumbent John Tippett in the 5-1 home mauling by Saffron Walden the previous Saturday could not have helped his cause.

Ely Crusaders managed a 0-0 draw at Blades, and the following week they advanced to the last eight of the League Cup again with a 3-1 home victory against Cambridge Hornets. In the meantime Ely City had appointed former central defender Roger Crane as their caretaker manager, and he named himself as substitute for the surprise 1-1 draw at Sudbury Town – only City's second point of the campaign.

Having come so close to relegation the previous season, Ely Crusaders found themselves just one point from the top of the Senior Division at the start of December 1983, but only three points off the bottom having played seven of their 18 fixtures. They could have gone top by winning away to champions Springbox in their next match, but were instead thrashed 9-1. The repercussions of that result were to be painfully felt on the final day of the season.

Ely City's 1983 Christmas came early with their first win since 6 November 1982 – again ironically, a 2-0 win at the expense of Thetford Town, although this time it was away from home. John 'Soapy' Edwards struck both goals, thus ending City's incredible run of 46 league games without winning.

I returned to Sunday action and helped Crusaders earn a 2-2 draw at Littlebury, and although we were still only four points off top spot we were worryingly only three points off the bottom. Ely City meanwhile moved off the foot of the Town & Country League table for the first time since September 1982 with a 2-0 win at Yarmouth – on 21 January 1984!

I was back on the Sunday scoresheet with a late goal in Crusaders' 4-2 reverse at Queens Arms, but we were having another good run in the League Cup and reached the last four again by winning 3-2 at Elsworth Sports after extra-time. This was a remarkable contest, because Elsworth – who had dispatched our Senior Division rivals Selser in the previous round – led 2-0 with 10 minutes of normal time remaining. I pulled a goal back with a downward header from Elliott Summers' cross however, and in the 88th minute a looping header from Marcus Humphry made it two each.

There was still time for the tie to go either way, as Humphry crossed just too high for his team-mates and goalkeeper Carl Thulborn saved bravely in a one-on-one situation. Volatile midfielder Summers was then dismissed in the 89th minute, meaning that we had to play the whole of extra-time a man short. Substitute Ian Bethell grabbed the winner for us in the second extra period though, slipping the ball past former Crusaders goalkeeper Alan Todd.

Back in the league we drew 0-0 at Sawston Keys, and now had only Exning United and BSC below us in the table. We failed to score again the following week, going down by the only goal of the game at home to Blades. I observed afterwards that if we finished below a team like Blades, then we would deserve to go down. Seven days later we entertained fellow strugglers Exning, and moved four points clear of them and six clear of BSC – who we still had to play twice – with a comprehensive 5-2 win in which I contributed our third goal.

Next we travelled to Selser, losing 4-1 with a very understrength line-up, Elliott Summers having been suspended until 26 March. Then came the League Cup semi-final clash with Springbox, which was decided during 25 first half minutes when the Cambridge side struck five times without reply. I pulled one back with a low pile-driver before the interval, but later missed a penalty as Springbox eventually progressed to the final 7-2 at our expense.

We then crumbled anonymously 4-0 in our first clash with BSC away from home, followed by an equally dismal 5-2 defeat by Girton Eagles on our own patch, meaning we had won only one league game in the last 11. BSC were already relegated by the time we beat them 4-1 at Downham Road, but we still needed to beat Selser at home in our final game, because Exning were only a point worse off than us with a superior goal difference. As it was, we could only draw 1-1 whilst Exning came from two goals down to beat Queens Arms 3-2, so we were relegated. I was so upset I couldn't even bring myself to write a match report.

CHAPTER FIFTEEN: Paradise Regained

A few years ago I went to a wedding in Soham which was followed by a reception at The Maltings in Ely, and amongst the guests were two former Sunday League defenders with whom I battled on many occasions. Phil Hubbard was one of them, but I will start with the conversation I began with Alan Barrett, in his day an uncompromising left full-back with Histon on Saturdays, and Girton Eagles on Sundays.

"It's Alan Barrett, isn't it?" I said as I approached him.

"You have me at a disadvantage," he replied in a manner so eloquent that it quite surprised me, "because I'm afraid I don't recognise you."

"I'm Steve Green," I said. "Midge. I used to play for Ely Crusaders."

"Yes, I remember you!" he smiled, "You had hair then! You were a tricky little bastard!"

So we renewed our acquaintance and chatted for a while about the players we both used to play with like Derek Waters, Peter Galenski and Bob Lyon, and we reminisced about the incredibly high standard of Sunday League football in the 'good old days'. Girton Eagles, Selser, Sawston Keys, Littlebury, Springbox, Phoenix, Hinton Rangers, BSC and of course Queens Arms were team names that sprang to mind in particular, all jam-packed with the cream of Cambridgeshire football. Players who had more than money on their minds.

I always relished my attempts to breach the Girton Eagles defence because I knew most of their players from Saturday football, but – with the exception of Selser – the one team I didn't look forward to facing was Burwell-based Queens Arms. Their central defenders were the supremely tough duo of Sean Kelly and Phil Hubbard, both well over six-feet tall, both superb in the air, and both very comfortable on the ground. If (as was often the case) you got no joy through the middle, you might be tempted out to the wing where gifted full backs such as the athletic Trevor Claxton were waiting to dispossess you or intercept a pass. I probably averaged less goals against Queens Arms than any other side in the Senior Division, and it was not difficult to see why.

Later in the evening Phil Hubbard and I got talking about football (as you do), and I mentioned the fact that he had played with semi-professional distinction for Cambridge City and Soham Town Rangers, had played for his home town side Burwell Swifts (winning the County League title), and had played many years for the Sunday League side Queens Arms. "Which football did you enjoy most?" I asked, fairly sure what his response would be.

"Queens Arms on Sundays," he said, "without a doubt."

The reason I mention this is to emphasise just how high the Senior Division standards were in Cambridgeshire Sunday football, and also to try to explain why I was so devastated when Ely Crusaders finally lost their place at Sunday League's top table at the end of the 1983/1984 season. Ironically, it had been the failure of Hubbard's Queens Arms to retain a two-goal lead against Exning United that had condemned us to the drop on goal difference.

Ely Crusaders' first match back in Division 1A at the start of the 1984/1985 Sunday League season resulted in a 3-2 defeat at Phoenix Reserves, a result which suggested that an immediate return to the top flight – by winning the Division - was highly improbable.

Before the 1984/1985 season had got underway I had travelled once again to St Hubert in Kempen, Germany, as a 'guest' player for Ely Park Rangers. In our match against the hosts we trailed 1-0, but got back on terms through Ashley Gwynn before I fired home the 2-1 winner. Prior to that we had played in an international tournament, drawing 1-1 with the team that eventually ran out winners. Although I was playing as a central defender I put us ahead from close range, but managed to cancel that out with an own goal header!

Back in England I had decided to leave Bury Town because Reserves manager Adrian Davies had left to work in America, so in September 1984 I once again signed for Ely City. My first game back was for the Reserves at Little Downham Swifts, and I thumped home a 'majestic' (not my words!) equaliser before we went down 3-1. The most notable aspect of the game however, was the fact that I managed to persuade the referee *not* to award us a penalty. Conditions were very wet, and in the first half my Ely Crusaders team-mate Alan Draper fouled me from behind. By the time I had finished my subsequent slide, I was well inside the penalty area so the referee whistled and pointed to the spot. I explained to him that I was outside the area when the offence was committed, and after consulting the home linesman he eventually changed his decision and awarded us a free-kick instead. My City Reserves' team-mates were perplexed, but I did at least earn a complimentary Ely Standard headline for my actions: *'No penalty, says sporting Steve.'* In the meantime City signed my former Cambridge City team-mate and one-time PE Teacher Tony Rule as assistant manager, coach and player.

I next scored the only goal of the game as Ely City Reserves won 1-0 at Barton Mills in Division 1B of the County League, but things were still not going well for Crusaders on Sundays and we suffered yet another league defeat, this time 6-3 at home to Barnwell. The following

Saturday I was back in Ely City's first team for the home match with Braintree Town, who were reigning Eastern Counties League champions at the time.

Geoff Seymour opened the scoring for us in the second minute, when my cracking volley was parried into his path by visiting goalkeeper Kelly. The Ely Standard newspaper later included the following in its report: *'Green impressed as Ely's best attacker. His sudden bursts, control at speed and willingness and ability to shoot hard, made him the one man the Irons' defence had to look out for.'* Braintree equalised, but: *'Green was always a danger and it took a great save by Kelly to stop him giving Ely the lead a few minutes before the interval.'* Instead Braintree went straight to the other end to go 2-1 in front before running out 4-1 winners, courtesy of a last minute penalty.

Beforehand – in midweek – we had travelled to play local rivals Soham Town Rangers, losing 2-1 in a match that manager Roger Crane described as "daylight robbery," this being the game that marked my return to Ely City's ranks following the season with Bury Town. The following week we lost 2-0 at windswept Newport Pagnell in the FA Vase, but on the Sunday Ely Crusaders returned to winning ways with an extra-time 4-3 Challenge Cup victory over Rose & Crown Alliance. I scored the goal which made it 3-3 at the end of normal time, and Marcus Humphry grabbed a dramatic late winner after Gary Dewey had missed a penalty.

At Ely City the following Saturday we drew 0-0 at home to fourth-placed Yarmouth Town, whilst on the Sunday Crusaders finally got their act together to collect their first points of the season at Manorians, with me scoring twice in a 5-2 success with a powerful first half header and a late tap-in.

When the next Saturday game came along, I earned the

headline *'Green Light'* for my performance in the home clash with Gorleston, and it was Ely City's first win over the 'Greens' since I had made my scoring debut in the 2-0 home win at the end of the 1976/1977 season. Winger Colin Anderson got behind the right side of the visiting defence in the 36th minute, and his cross enabled me to glide a first-time shot past the 'keeper for the only goal of the afternoon. In the next 'Robins' game at Sudbury I hit the bar with a snap-shot and tested their goalkeeper in the second half, but we were undone by two goals in the last 10 minutes to eventually lose 3-0.

After a 2-1 League Cup Second Round defeat for Crusaders at Queens Arms I was unfit for Ely City's 3-0 loss at Harwich, due to the aforementioned mystery foot injury I had suffered walking to work one morning. I was therefore unable to play in my usual outfield position in the Sunday Challenge Cup Second Round tie at Forest Rangers, but did play as an emergency goalkeeper instead! Although I wrote the match report myself, I don't think I exaggerated when I stated that I had *'denied the hosts with spectacular and unorthodox saves.'* Forest Rangers finally made the breakthrough in the first period of extra-time, and struck again in the second to claim a richly deserved 2-0 win.

Ely City's Centenary Year began in 1985, but I remained on the sidelines with that frustrating mystery foot injury. It was at the beginning of this year however, that I took over as Junior Football reporter for the new-look Ely Standard newspaper, and 'Steve Green's Junior Scene' was to remain a feature of the Ely Standard sports pages for more than 20 years. I was offered £5 per week at the start, but managed to negotiate £13 instead. This had risen to £90 per week by the time I ultimately lost the job due to recessionary influences; the Standard could not attract advertising, so it could no longer afford to pay freelancers like me. I was absolutely gutted, because I loved the work and had formed many close friendships with contributors who were involved in local football.

In the early days I handwrote my reports, and they were subsequently typed up by Pam Knighton who was the wife of the Sports Editor, Brian Knighton. Computer technology consigned typewriters to the dustbin however, so in due course I was placing copy straight on to the system myself. This was fine with me because I had learned to touch-type at school (gaining an RSA Stage 2 pass with distinction, but failing the Advanced Stage 3). When the newspaper decided to cut staff during the recession I even took on the Sports Editor's job for a few months (at £120 per week), but there were strict Tuesday deadlines to meet and I found it increasingly difficult to fit the role in with my full-time job as a Tax Inspector. It was something of a relief when the Editor decided to end the arrangement.

Although I briefly returned to compile the Junior Football column again, I knew the writing was on the wall and that in due course my writing would no longer feature on the local sports pages. I had also provided copy intermittently to the Norwich Green 'Un and the Ipswich Pink 'Un football papers, but that finished too and soon afterwards my days as a part-time journalist were yesterday's news.

Back on the field I played in goal again for Ely Crusaders in their final game of the season, conceding two second half goals as Soham Town Rangers came back from 2-0 down to salvage an away draw. My Saturday club Ely City meanwhile finished on 31 points from their 42 Town & Country League games by virtue of a 1-1 draw against champions Braintree, a result which meant that they were almost certainly safe from re-election (by avoiding finishing in the bottom two). The three teams immediately below them – Newmarket Town, Harwich and Haverhill Rovers – still had games to play and all three teams could hypothetically overtake them, but it was a highly unlikely scenario.

Newmarket had two games left and were one point behind, but had a worse goal difference. Harwich had one game left and were also one point behind with an inferior goal difference. Likewise Haverhill had one game left, but were two points behind with a worse goal difference. Haverhill would have had to beat Newmarket 5-0 to overtake Ely, Harwich would have had to beat Wisbech Town, and then Newmarket would have had to beat Tiptree United in their final outing to overhaul City as well. (I hope you followed all that). As it was, Newmarket and Haverhill drew with each other, and Newmarket and Harwich lost their final matches, so Ely finished with four teams below them in the table.

CHAPTER SIXTEEN: The End of the 'Crusades'

'Chic' Cooper eventually relinquished the managerial role at Ely Crusaders after one pretty dreadful season in Division 1A during which I had mostly been sidelined, and I – perhaps by default – took over as the 1985/1986 player-manager in an attempt to return us to the top flight. I knew it wasn't going to be easy, because you had to win the Division to gain promotion and decent teams like Swaffham United, Soham Town Rangers and Mildenhall Social Club were always going to make that difficult.

Full-back Richard Goodjohn disappointingly changed his allegiance to Queens Arms, but his young cousin Gary Goodjohn came on board and central defender Richard Lant joined us too, along with midfielder Terry Stone and striker Andy Day. I was optimistic about our chances, and we began the season in style, winning our first three league outings 7-2, 6-1 and 8-0 against Brooklands United, Newmarket Exning Road Athletic and Phoenix Reserves respectively before dumping Senior Division hosts Barnwell out of the Sunday Challenge Cup 4-2 after extra-time.

A dismal 5-2 league defeat at Exning United seemed like a mere blip at the time, and a 6-0 League Cup thrashing of Ida Darwin was soon followed by a superb 4-3 Challenge Cup quarter-final victory over mighty Queens Arms. Soham-based Angle Rangers were the next visitors to a very wet and windy Downham Road, and although I contributed a hat-trick we were ultimately held to a 4-4 draw. One of my goals that day was scored against the wind, when my header would have fallen short of the goal-line, but the ball hit a puddle in the six-yard box and skipped past the startled goalkeeper!

My run of six successive scoring appearances came to an

end as Histon United dumped us out of the League Cup 3-2 at home, but Andy Day scored the only goal of the game in a 1-0 league win at Local Exams and I was back on the goal-trail with four more in away victories at Mildenhall Social Club (3-1), Soham Town Rangers (3-2) and Brooklands United (5-2).

Andy Day again grabbed the only goal as Rose & Crown Reliance were beaten 1-0 at home in a drab semi-final of the Challenge Cup, and I took my personal tally to 16 in 15 league and cup matches with a brace in the 5-2 victory over Local Exams. Our next few games were crucial, and in the first of them – the final of the Challenge Cup at Christchurch – we were edged out 2-1 by Whittlesey-based Bricklayers Arms in the windiest conditions imaginable.

With the elements in their favour we felt we had done well to hold them to 1-0 at the interval, and when Terry Stone fired in off the underside of the bar to equalise we thought that the trophy was ours for the taking. With practically their only attack of the second half however, Bricklayers grabbed a bizarre second goal and we were unable to retrieve the deficit.

Our next league match at Soham Town Rangers was played away because our ground was waterlogged, and as it happened we suffered a damaging 5-3 defeat which meant that we needed to win all our remaining games to have any chance of winning the title. A brilliant Alan Moore-inspired 5-0 win over Mildenhall set us up for the visit of leaders Swaffham United the following week, but they deservedly beat us 2-1 and our challenge was over. I scored my 17th and 18th goals of the season in the 5-3 home win against Exning United, but that victory was sandwiched by a dismal 7-0 defeat at Angle Rangers in which I fluffed a penalty, and a 5-0 loss at Swaffham United which clinched the title for them ahead of a bitterly disappointed Mildenhall Social Club, whose two losses to us had cost them dearly.

The season had fizzled out tamely for us after the Challenge Cup final, and I was – not for the first time – a little disappointed with the commitment of certain players at crucial times of the season. Maybe I expected too much of them and clearly they didn't care about the club or indeed Sunday football as much as I did, but the fact remains that few of them were interested when it came to putting the nets up, sweeping the dressing rooms or raising money to keep the club going, and with that in mind I made the decision to end my 13-year association with Ely Crusaders Football Club. I had played precisely 100 league games for the first team, scoring 87 goals, and in 30 Cup ties I had found the net 27 times.

After 101 years at the Paradise Sports Ground, it had been announced in June 1985 that Ely City would be relocating in 1986, moving – somewhat ironically – to Downham Road Playing Fields in September of that year. Trevor Moden and Gary Grogan in the meantime returned to Ely City for the start of the 1985/1986 season, along with another striker Malcolm Campbell who arrived from Cherry Hinton. City completed an unbeaten five match build-up to the new season, but went on to lose their first seven Town & Country League fixtures which prompted the departure (yet again) of Moden and Grogan to Soham Town Rangers and Cambridge City respectively. Grogan had just scored the solitary extra-time goal in Ely's Preliminary Round FA Vase victory over Lowestoft Town.

On 7 September 1985 I finally returned to action for Ely City Reserves in Division 1B, scoring four goals in our opening day 5-0 demolition of Camden Reserves. In those days I never mentioned my own name in the reports for matches I was involved in, but having got wind of my four-goal haul Ely Standard Sports Editor Brian Knighton wrote a paragraph under the heading: *'Modest Steve.'* He went on to say that *'It is never easy to write about yourself as I have discovered when attempting to report my occasional minor triumphs at bowls. So modesty prevented Steve Green reporting his four goals for Ely Reserves on Saturday. So I have done it for him. Well done, Steve. It's good to have you back in action with your boots as well as your pen.'*

The following Saturday however, I was again thoroughly disillusioned by the abject manner in which we surrendered 2-0 at Lode and therefore made the decision that being a player-manager on Sundays was enough to contend with for the time being.

City Reserves proceeded to win each of their next eight league matches, so clearly they didn't miss me that much! Ironically it was for the return clash with Lode that I was tempted to rejoin the Reserves, and with the score standing at 1-1 I thumped in a last-minute header from a corner off the underside of the crossbar to secure a ninth successive league win.

Now back in the first team however, I teamed up with Richard Palmer for the first time in our careers and he set me up for the opening goal in our Town & Country League match at Chatteris Town. Home defender Mark Deighton then broke my nose with his elbow, but I stayed on to provide the last minute cross for Nigel Fuller to head home our second before making my way to hospital to have my snout (partially) straightened. Deighton didn't like it much because although he was well over six-feet tall I repeatedly beat him in the air. I upset many defenders in that way because they felt that height was the key to being good in the air. It isn't; it is timing that matters most.

Our next match was in midweek at Wisbech Town, and in the 37th minute their central defender Mel Matless miskicked completely and I was through on goal. As the goalkeeper attempted to narrow the angle I coolly placed a left-foot shot past his right hand and just inside the post, putting us ahead before we eventually went down 2-1. I didn't know it at the time, but it would be my 44th and last ever goal for the Robins (although not my last ever goal at Fenland Park).

In fairness to me the first 38 of those goals came in my first 99 appearances for the club, 10 of which were as substitute. It is abundantly clear that the departure of player-manager Lester Newell signalled the end of my 'heyday' at Ely City, coinciding as it did with the unfortunate 'Mayday!' appointments of John Tippett and then Ted Robbins.

A 0-0 draw at Bury Town was followed by a 1-0 win at Harwich in the First Round Proper of the FA Vase. I set up Richard Palmer for the only goal of the game 12 minutes from time, and this earned us a Second Round home clash with the previous season's semi-finalists – Wisbech Town. In the Town & Country League Cup we didn't fare so well, losing 2-1 at home to March, but this was followed by a commendable 1-1 league draw away to leaders Sudbury Town.

In the Cambs Invitation Cup we were drawn away to Cambridge City, and I was injured by a tackle from behind early in the game which we eventually lost 3-1. Damaged ankle ligaments meant that I missed the 2-1 home defeat by Harwich and the 3-1 victory at Newmarket, and I was also unavailable for the FA Vase clash with Wisbech which ended 2-2 after extra-time. Wisbech won the replay 5-0, and I returned to action in the 5-2 setback at home to Colchester Reserves. Unfortunately I only lasted 20 minutes before my ankle ligaments gave way again, and my Ely City first team days were over for the time being*.

I subsequently did make an attempt to break into the Robins First Team again some years later, when they were managed by former Cambridge United and Northern Ireland player Tom Finney and by which time they had been relegated to the newly-formed Jewson League Division One. Ely were at the top of the league and goals from Karl Simper were helping to keep them there, so I bided my time on the bench. I thought my chance had come when Simper was unavailable for the home clash with Mildenhall Town, but Finney paraded new signing Mel Pryer in the dressing room before the game and he was in the starting line-up instead of me. I walked out but – after calming down and playing the final 20 minutes of the match – never had anything to do with Ely City again. During the game I collected the ball in midfield and hit one of my best shots ever - straight into the brick-built dug-out where Finney and his assistant Roger Crane were sitting! The ball cannoned around them like a pinball and the looks on their faces were priceless!

Returning to the 1985/1986 season, Ely City Reserves had earned a 2-0 Junior Cup quarter-final victory at St Andrews, but had no goalkeeper available for the top-of-the-table clash at Cambridge University Press. So despite my ongoing injury, I stepped into the breach and produced several decent saves as we claimed an unlikely 2-0 win. I was not fit (and our recognised goalkeeper was back) as we were thrashed 5-0 at home by the same opponents the following week, but we reached the Junior Cup Final without having conceded a goal, dispatching Waterbeach Reserves 3-0 in the semi-final. Fordham were then beaten 2-1 in the league before we slumped to a 3-1 defeat after extra-time in the final of the Junior Cup against our main rivals Cambridge University Press.

The hangover to that defeat was a 2-0 setback at Isleham

United, but Coleridge and Waterbeach Reserves were overcome by six-goal margins in successive weeks and we were left with an unbelievable five matches in eight days to clinch the Division 1B title. On the assumption that Press would win their remaining games, we knew that we needed a minimum of seven points from a possible 10 to win the league on goal difference, but the first four of those remaining games were away from home.

We won 4-0 at Little Downham on the Saturday, but Waterbeach Reserves held us 3-3 on the Tuesday evening and Wicken Amateurs beat us 3-1 the following night with me in goal. On the Thursday night we won 5-0 at Eastern Gas, so that left us with Barton Mills to defeat at home on the final Saturday of the season. They established an early lead, but I was amongst the scorers as we eventually ran out 4-1 winners to claim the title.

Andy Day struck the only goal of the game to win the Division One play-off against Abington, but that season for Ely City Reserves really belonged to the ageing John 'Soapy' Edwards, who helped himself to 21 goals in all competitions. I fully intended to stay at the club for 1986/1987, but many players – including me – left the Reserves simply because nobody bothered to contact them at the start of the campaign, so initially I signed for no-one.

CHAPTER SEVENTEEN: 'Manny'

Soham Town Rangers Reserves player-manager Mick 'Manny' Robinson recruited my Ely Park Rangers colleague Ashley Gwynn to play up front at the start of the 1986/1987 season, with 'Ash' having scored 31 league and cup goals for Division 4B Sutton United the previous season. He grabbed a couple of braces for Soham in the opening six Premier Division B games, but things were not really working out for either him or the team, so 'Manny' approached me with a view to replacing him. Rangers had taken just three points from a possible 14 at that stage, and on my debut at Over Sports I did not help to improve that record as we suffered an unlucky 3-0 defeat.

Our next match was at home to fellow strugglers Littleport Town, and I grabbed my first goal for Rangers in a comfortable 8-2 win. We then travelled to title-chasing Trumpington, and although we managed to win I remember the match mostly for the worst miss of my entire career. The ball was played towards the near post and the Trumpington 'keeper went to the corner of his six-yard box to gather the ball. Somehow he let it slip through his grasp and through his legs, and as I was standing directly behind him I found the ball at my feet, facing an unguarded goal which was just one yard away. But for some reason I just couldn't seem to move my legs, and ended up prodding the ball pathetically to one side. A defender rushed in to clear, but my embarrassment was short-lived because Graham Eley immediately played the ball back into the six-yard box and I was on hand to score with a powerful left-foot volley. My subsequent direct free-kick sealed a 3-1 victory for us.

We went out of the Challenge Cup at the first hurdle and lost 3-1 in the league at Orwell, but a record of 32 points from a possible 36 since the defeat at Over Sports had put us on the fringe of the promotion race. Cottenham then beat us 2-1 at home, but 11 points out of a possible 12 just about kept us in the hunt and we needed to beat league leaders Trumpington to sustain our challenge for the runners-up berth.

It was a very tight game, and midway through the second half Graham Eley lofted a pass towards the edge of the Trumpington penalty area. I was running alongside a defender, but out of the corner of my eye saw goalkeeper Richard Powis advancing well off his line. So instead of trying to bring the drifting ball down, I stooped and nodded it upwards – over the stranded goalkeeper and into an empty net. Unfortunately the visitors hit back with two quick goals to claim the points, but in the bar after the game Powis came up to me and asked me if I meant to score with the header. I said that I did because I saw him coming off his line, but it was quite apparent from his reaction that he didn't believe me!

I think it was a good example of what I often describe as 'spatial awareness'. Whenever I played, I was somehow always aware of what was happening in the 360 degrees around me. As 'Chic' always maintained, when the ball is coming towards you its trajectory is unlikely to change, so during its flight you invariably have time to assess what is happening around you, or indeed what is likely to happen or what you want to happen when the ball reaches you. So with the Trumpington goal, I ran forward but looked behind me to see Graham Eley strike the ball. I gauged the trajectory and then made an instant assessment of what was happening around me. Defender on my left shoulder. No other players nearby. Ball travelling towards the area above my right shoulder. Goalkeeper advancing beyond the penalty spot. Consider options. Head it wider and re-assess position? Try to hold the ball up and wait for support? Lob header into empty goal. It all happened in an instant, but as you can see the process takes a lot longer than that to describe!

We finished the season in third spot having taken 34 points from a possible 44 since I joined the club and I ended up with 15 goals, whilst my strike partner Alan Moore helped himself to 20. Alan reverted to a central defensive role in the season that followed however, so it was left to me and the rejuvenated Richard Palmer to spearhead the attack in the 1987/1988 season.

Richard had struggled with his confidence during the 1986/1987 campaign, managing only six goals in all competitions. After five scoreless games in the following season however, he became more like his old self and we formed a quite lethal partnership.

Fifteen league and cup matches passed without defeat, and the only points we dropped were at Orwell and Fulbourn Reserves. I had 18 goals to my credit at this stage, and Richard was close behind with 16. The last of those 15 games was at Foxton, who were struggling badly at the time and turned up with only nine players. Incredibly they took a 2-0 lead before we regained our composure and eventually ran out 12-3 winners!

Gamlingay were also unbeaten at this point in time, and they were the next visitors to Julius Martin Lane for a midweek clash under the floodlights. It turned out to be quite an eventful game, and it was my first encounter with a defender who I will simply refer to as 'The Moron.'

'The Moron' was as brainless as he was ugly, and as I stood on the halfway line waiting for the ball to be cleared from our penalty area he simply walked up to me and kicked me on the back of the leg. I angrily pushed him away and asked him in no uncertain terms what the hell he thought he was up to, at which point the referee intervened. I doubt that 'The Moron' understood what the ref was saying because there were too many syllables involved, so the physical abuse continued throughout the game and I received virtually no protection.

I got more and more frustrated as the game progressed, but with 20 minutes remaining we won a corner and when the cross came in I got to the ball first, nodding it downwards. The goalkeeper Andy Brookman should perhaps have saved my effort, but he allowed it to slip through his grasp and the ball was over the line before anyone could clear it. In the closing stages Richard Palmer got to the bye-line and pulled the ball back for me to drive home a second, making the final score 2-0 and ending Gamlingay's unbeaten record in the process.

We looked like we were destined to be champions after this win, but were in for a rude awakening in our next match away to struggling Earith United.

We were trailing 4-2 by the time I scored a consolation penalty kick that reduced the final deficit to a single goal, but in the first half I had contributed one of the most bizarre goals of my entire career. A loose ball fell in the middle of the Earith six-yard box and I dived forward, hoping to get my head to it but fearing that a defender's boot would get to my head first. Initially I failed to connect with anything, but as I did a forward roll the bouncing ball clipped my studs and somehow flew into the top left-hand corner of the net behind me!

This defeat by a poor Earith side seemed to dent our confidence, and the following week we dropped our first home points of the season, losing 2-0 to Camden. It was also the first time we had failed to score since my debut at Over Sports the previous season – a run of 40 matches and 129 goals. Our form remained unimpressive as we won 1-0 at Bottisham and drew 2-2 at Ashley Magpies, and although I returned to scoring ways in the 3-1 home win against Fulbourn Reserves the same scoreline saw us defeated at Swavesey*. After three defeats in six matches the advantage in the title race was now firmly with Gamlingay.

> *I remember the first time I played at Swavesey's dump, because when I arrived there I desperately needed a dump! When I asked for the location of the toilet, I was duly informed that there wasn't one, so I had no option but to do my business in a nearby ditch. However, the first thing I needed to consider was the second thing I would be doing – wiping my arse. My only option was to buy several strips of cloakroom (draw) tickets from a Swavesey official, and use those. I never did find out if I won anything.*

I next scored the opener in a 2-0 Cambs Challenge Cup Second Round home win over Ashley Magpies, kicking off a run of nine successive victories in all competitions. I was on target again as Orwell were thrashed 5-0 at Julius Martin Lane, and again with a neat shot on the turn as we won 4-2 at Cambridge University Press. Next up was Premier Division Pye in the last eight of the Cambs Challenge Cup, again at our place. My goal kept us on level terms during normal time, and I went on to complete my hat-trick as our much-fancied opponents finished on the wrong end of a 4-1 scoreline.

A Gary Chilvers goal was enough for us to beat St Andrews 1-0 in our next home league game, but we again required extra-time to overcome Great Shelford Reserves away from home in the semi-final of the William Cockell Cup, Richard Palmer's double seeing us through by a 2-1 margin. The games were coming thick and fast for us as we stayed on course for the treble, and a midweek visit to windswept Abington was always going to be difficult. I scored our opener with the elements in our favour, but the hosts looked dangerous in the second half and our 2-0 interval lead was soon cut in half. Then came one of the most freakish goals I have ever witnessed.

In a rare attack, Andy Parker fired a shot into the wind from the edge of the Abington penalty area. The ball hit the underside of the bar but bounced down about a yard the wrong side of the line. Just at that moment, the wind dropped and the ball was literally 'sucked' into the Abington net to put us 3-1 up! The 'Dubious Goals' panel would perhaps have given it as an own goal to God! In any event, Abington pulled another goal back but were beaten 3-2.

Next was the Cambs Challenge Cup semi-final at Leverington Sports. They were a top side in the Peterborough League and we knew it would be a very tough encounter. The home side were on the receiving end of a very early shock however, as a corner from Graham Eley went straight into the net at the near post. We were very solid at the back that day, and Leverington struggled to make inroads despite having the majority of possession. Then on the break I took the ball into the left side of the Leverington area and squared a pass which Paul Giddens clipped home with a deft first-time shot. 2-0, game over.

Another midweek trip saw me grab the winner as Willingham were beaten 2-1, but I was absent the following Saturday as Soham Town Reserves travelled to Gamlingay. When I phoned for the result 'Manny' told me that the team had played well, but had lost 5-0! Our promotion hopes were still alive, but it now looked certain that we would not be promoted as champions. The defeat was quickly followed by the William Cockell Cup Final at Histon, where once again we faced our arch rivals Gamlingay. We were by far the better side, but fell behind in the first half and never managed to retrieve the situation.

How I didn't (at least) get booked in that final I will never know. I was fired up simply by virtue of the fact that I was facing 'The Moron' again, and after I had committed a series of fouls (not just on him) he attempted to wrestle me from behind at the start of the second half. He made the mistake of putting his misshapen head under my arm however, so I dragged him from the edge of his own penalty area to the edge of the centre-circle and then threw him to the ground. I later rattled a 20-yard shot against the underside of the crossbar, but that was as close as we came and the trophy undeservedly went back to Gamlingay.

The final nail in our Premier Division B title coffin came in the shape of a 3-1 defeat at home to Earith, who thus became the only team to do the double over us that season. The penalty I scored in that game was scant consolation, but I struck again in the 2-0 win at Camden and then grabbed a hat-trick – including a penalty – in the last league game of the season, a 6-2 defeat of Papworth. In the penultimate game we had won 1-0 at Great Shelford Reserves, but it was of little consequence because we knew we had finished second anyway.

Our last chance to secure any silverware was the final of the Cambs Challenge Cup at Newmarket, where we faced Great Shelford's mighty first team from the Premier Division, and took an early lead through Richard Palmer – his 27th goal of the campaign. Shelford gradually got their act together however, and managed to establish a 3-1 advantage. A last minute penalty award enabled me to reduce the deficit to one with my 37th goal of the season, but it was too late to salvage the tie so we had finished runners-up in everything!

CHAPTER EIGHTEEN: Another bad break

Soham Town Rangers Reserves looked capable of doing well in the Premier Division, and our first two results certainly supported that view. In our midweek opener at home to Fulbourn Institute we overcame a two-goal interval deficit to take the points 3-2, and on the Saturday we entertained Philips UK (formerly Pye, who we had beaten in the previous season's Challenge Cup quarter-final). Again we fell behind, and although Johnny Fretwell equalised we were 2-1 in arrears at the break.

At the start of the second half we pressed forward in search of the equaliser, and when I swung over a curling right-footed cross from the left wing it looked as if we had got it. The goalposts at Soham had large stanchions which curved from the back of the crossbar to about half-way down each post. My cross was unreachable and the ball flew beneath the crossbar in the far corner before cannoning off the stanchion a yard behind the line, ballooning upwards and back out onto the pitch. It was clearly a goal, but for some reason the referee simply played on. I ran up to him and asked him how it was physically possible for the ball to have cannoned upwards off the post (because it clearly didn't hit the bar), but he was having none of it and threatened to book me instead!

Soon afterwards I went up for a header about 25 yards from the Philips goal-line, and when I landed I knew I had suffered a serious injury to my left foot. I leaned forward with my hands on my thighs and grimaced as the visiting sweeper collected the ball and attempted to find a team-mate to his right. As the ball passed in front of me I instinctively stuck out my injured left foot and stopped it. In the same movement I planted my right foot and lashed in a low diagonal drive with my broken left. The ball nestled in the bottom right-hand corner to make the score

2-2, and I immediately limped off the pitch with what proved to be a stress-fracture! Fretwell grabbed his second goal of the game to clinch another 3-2 victory, but the 'broken foot goal' was my last ever for Soham Town Rangers Reserves, and my last meaningful appearance for the side (although I did start three more games in the early months of 1989). Up to and including that match against Philips UK, I had scored 53 goals in 54 appearances for Rangers.

By the time I had recovered from the stress-fracture of my left foot, Mick 'Manny' Robinson was manager of the first team at Soham Town Rangers. I had previously refused to play for the first team that season under Johnny Fretwell because I felt that he had made little effort to recruit players in the close season, hoping instead that the Reserve players would step into a breach they mostly had no real desire to fill. Johnny and I had a very public spat via my column in the newspaper, and whilst I appreciated his view that all players at the club should be prepared to play for the first team, I did not believe that many of the Reserve players would have joined or stayed at the club on that understanding.

However, when 'Manny' took over the reins he wanted to know if I would play first team football at Soham, and I responded by saying that he was one of only two managers I would be prepared to do that for ('Chic' Cooper being the other). The first game was a midweek visit to Wisbech, where I was the consolation scorer in a 4-1 defeat – the third time I had scored on my debut for a club in the Eastern Counties league. I could be wrong, but I think it was the last time I ever played alongside Trevor Moden. Next up was a trip to Brantham, where I hit the post during a rather unlucky 2-1 defeat.

In the subsequent home clash with Harwich, I opened the scoring for Rangers after intercepting an under hit back-pass by my former Bury Town colleague Murray Osman, and although the visitors equalised a spectacular volleyed goal by my former Ely Crusaders team-mate Elliott Summers earned us a 2-1 win. That was as good as it got for 'Manny' and me however; he lost his job and – at the age of only 28 – I was destined never to score again at that level.

Towards the end of the 1988/1989 season I played twice for Soham Town Rangers 'A,' scoring three times. I also netted three goals in as many appearances for Ely Park Rangers, helping them (belatedly) to lift the Division 2A title on Sundays. Ely were unbeaten in the league with six matches remaining, but their next match was against Fordham Crown Rangers who were also undefeated. Fordham only had a couple of fixtures left, so all they had to do to secure the title was avoid defeat against us. My assigned role in the game was to nullify the effectiveness of their brilliant midfielder Darren Theobald.

I carried out my task particularly well that day, and Theobald was restricted to one long range effort which our goalkeeper Steve Woods dealt with fairly comfortably. But a draw was not enough, so in the closing stages I moved forward behind what was a comparatively rare attack for us. Ashley Gwynn managed to get to the touchline on the right side of the penalty box, and I called for him to cut the ball back to the edge of the area. As defenders closed in on me I knew I would have only one chance to score, so I connected first time with a low, powerful left-foot drive. I don't know if my effort would have been saved or not, but the shot took the slightest deflection off the bottom of an outstretched defender's leg and flew into the corner beneath the goalkeeper's right hand for the only goal of the game.

We duly won our remaining five games to lift the Division 2A title, and then won the Division Two play-off with a gritty performance against an aggressive Haymakers side. Ashley Gwynn opened the scoring from the penalty spot, and his brother Robert made it 2-0 before the Cambridge side pulled one back.

Two years prior to that I had made four appearances for the club's Reserves, scoring seven times including a hat-trick when we lost 7-3 at home to Newmarket Albion Reserves. I remember that game in particular because it was the only competitive game I ever played with nearly all of my mates from Ely, most of whom did not play regular football (hence the scoreline)!

In the season that followed I played very little local football. My five Sunday matches for Ely Park Rangers yielded six goals, and my seven matches for Ely City Reserves produced six goals – including a hat-trick against Eastern Gas that was recorded on video tape. It was a terrible game in truth, played in bone-hard, dusty conditions, but I scored with my right foot, left foot and then with a powerful header to help us on the way to a 5-1 success. Having lost four of their first six league matches however, City went unbeaten for the remainder of the season and finished runners-up in Division 2B of the County League, thus gaining promotion back to Division 1B.

The following season (1990/1991) I played more regularly for Ely City Reserves, scoring 21 goals in 20 appearances in all competitions plus one more in a solitary appearance for the 'A' team. A 22-match unbeaten run in all competitions – including 20 victories – came to an end when Somersham Reserves beat us 2-1 at home, but we finished high up the table and I do recall scoring with a half-volley from the halfway line in the win at Isleham!

In 1991/1992 I made only 12 appearances for Ely City Reserves, scoring six times. Four of those goals came in the Creake Shield, in which four matches took us to a last four place that was ultimately denied us by Derek Oakey's failure to send off the registration form for Andy Day. As the years passed, my appearances in local football became even more sporadic. Just nine games for Ely Park Rangers in 1992/1993 (four league goals) and a mere two matches for Ely Park Rangers Reserves in 1993/1994 (one league goal). So in seven seasons, I had played just 65 games in local football, finding the net 53 times. At the start of the 1994/1995 season however, I joined Division 2B side Littleport Town, and things were about to take a turn for the better.

CHAPTER NINETEEN: 'Port in a Storm

Recently-appointed player-manager Gary Chilvers invited me to play for Littleport Town in the 1994/1995 season, and I was pleased to join my former Ely Crusaders teammate in his attempt to revive the fortunes of his hometown club. I opened my account with a hat-trick in the 4-0 demolition of local rivals Little Downham Swifts, and added 12 more league goals as the season progressed for a total of 15 in as many appearances as we clinched the Division 2B championship ahead of Somersham Town 'A.'

The following season (1995/1996) things started reasonably well in Division 1B with Terry Stone now at the helm and four points from three games (including two goals for me), but the 1-1 draw at Wicken Amateurs prompted me to quit the team. In the previous game – a thrilling 4-4 draw at home to Somersham 'A' in which I opened the scoring – new signing Mark Smith had come on as substitute and had made a significant impact, scoring the last two goals to salvage a point as we came back from 4-1 down. I was aware of Mark's reputation for selfish play from his Stretham Hotspurs days however, and it didn't take me long to realise that I would not enjoy playing in the same team as him. About 100 minutes to be precise.

I therefore left the club, explaining that there was no way I could play in the same team as Mark Smith. His flame burned brightly and briefly before its inevitable extinguishment, and I rejoined the club in mid-season when it was under new management and Mark had gone. I scored from a great free-kick move in the 1-1 draw at Milton (against my old chum Ian Smith) and then scored with a scissor-kick volley in the 5-1 win at Somersham 'A', but the new manager Mr Dodman took himself too seriously for football at that level for my liking and I could not tolerate his ultra-critical approach. Consequently I left Littleport Town FC for the second time that season, but did however rejoin the club for a third time after a short period away (about 17 years to be precise, aged 52)!

In 1996/1997 I played a few Sunday games for Ely Crusaders, opening my 'new' account in the 4-2 'home' win over Ely Park Rangers (both teams were located at the Paradise Sports Ground). The following Sunday we lost 3-0 at home to Kingston Foresters Reserves, but the only reason I remember this is because it was the morning Princess Diana died. I strained a hamstring in that game, but returned for the 1-0 Junior Cup victory against Barnwell when I scored the only goal of the game with a late penalty. In our next match – the Third Round of the same competition – we were drawn away to NCI Musketeers, who were undoubtedly the strongest side remaining. After going two goals down, we pulled one back at the start of the second half when the ball was laid up to the edge of the Musketeers' penalty area. I managed to nip in front of the nearest defender, and fired an acute-angled drive across the goalkeeper and inside the far post to make it 2-1. We had chances to equalise, but couldn't take them and NCI scored again to clinch the tie. My final ever goal for Ely Crusaders came the following Sunday in the home clash with Exning United, when we were beaten 5-2.

I started the 1997/1998 season back at Ely Park Rangers, scoring twice (once with my knee) in the 4-2 reverse at Jockey Giants in the Sunday League Cup and once in the 4-1 success at Swaffham United in the Junior Cup. Otherwise I seldom played at all as Rangers gained promotion from Division 2A by finishing runners-up. In 1998/1999 they finished third in Division 1A, and although I played fairly regularly then it was as a central defender and I contributed just three league goals.

The following season I accompanied the Reserves on a trip to Brinkley Red Lion, heading in a consolation goal as we capitulated 8-1. I was so disgusted with the attitude of the players that I left the club and signed instead for Witchford. I quickly progressed from the Reserves to the first team, and with the latter reached the final of the Junior Cup – only to be thrown out once again following an administrative error by the Club Secretary (not Derek Oakey on this occasion!)

Back at Ely Park Rangers in 2000/2001, I struck four goals from central defence during a relatively poor campaign. In 2001/2002 however – at the age of 41 – I picked up my second ever Player-of-the-Year award – 24 years after the first, and my only one ever outside the ranks of Youth Football.

After opening the season with a 6-1 win at Brinkley Red Lion, we lost successive games at Wicken Maids Head (4-0) and Frank Lee Centre (1-0). I played pretty well in the second of those matches, and even better as the lone scorer in a 2-1 defeat at Fulbourn Institute. We were 2-0 down in the second half when I scored one of the more unusual goals of my career. I had pushed forward from defence, when – 20 minutes from time – a pass came into the penalty area from the left wing. 15 yards from goal, I controlled the ball with my right foot and pushed it to my left foot. With my route to goal blocked, I then pushed it to my right again and then back to my left. Whilst in the process of shuffling the ball from right to left, the Fulbourn captain audibly commented that I would "never score from there". When the ball finally moved from my left foot to my right and back to my left again for the last time, I unleashed a first-time half-volley which flew past the 'keeper and high into the right-hand corner of the net. The Fulbourn captain's next comment was: "Fuck me, he has."

Owing to my 'striking appearance' (ha, ha) in the Fulbourn game, I started up front in our fifth successive away game at Studlands Park. Opening the scoring with a bludgeoning far post header, I subsequently put us 2-1 in front with a remarkable goal. Roger Rich clipped the ball into the area when he saw my forward run, and as the ball dropped over my shoulder I saw the goalkeeper coming off his line and jumped to execute a high-kicking side-foot volley. When the 'keeper saw the ball drifting over his head and into the far corner of the net, he was only eight yards off his line. At the time the initial pass was made, I think he could envisage himself clattering me big time on the edge of the area.

Moments later Roger was again in the thick of the action, crossing from the right to enable me to complete my hat-trick with a thumping header into the top right-hand corner. Our 3-2 interval lead was increased to 4-2 when I won a penalty early in the second half and Roger converted, but we sat back on our laurels and Studlands hit back strongly to run out 5-4 winners on the day.

I was on target again in the 3-1 Millennium Cup defeat of Barnwell, and scored once again in the 5-2 home reverse at the hands of Frank Lee Centre. We therefore looked in deep trouble with just three points to our credit and five successive league defeats to our name, but things turned around with consecutive away wins at Witchford Reserves (5-2) and QPR Ely (3-2). We then entertained Brinkley Red Lion expecting a third win in a row, but it took us ages to break them down. Brian Halliwell – who was well over 50 at the time – finally broke the deadlock with a very clever finish after I had dummied a pass from my younger namesake Steve Green, and I then made it 2-0 with a firm header from Gary Dewsbury's corner kick. I failed to score in the four games that followed, but found the net direct with a 'boomerang' of a corner in the 4-4 draw at windswept Phoenix. Mark Hills grabbed all four goals in the 4-1 win at Isleham-based JEB, and we then entertained a Witchford Reserves side that turned up with only nine players. The visitors went ahead and were still in front five minutes before the interval, but my stooping far-post header from a corner put us back on terms and Gary Dewsbury put us ahead before half-time. The second period was inevitably one-way traffic, and I completed my hat-trick with two utterly contrasting goals.

For the first one I was on the edge of the six-yard box when the ball bounced high towards me. From a standing position, I headed the ball back diagonally and upwards, effectively lobbing the goalkeeper. For the second I was clean through and tried (like the old days) to glide the ball into the bottom right-hand corner. Instead the ball flew off my right boot and went just underneath the crossbar into the top corner! It looked impressive, but in truth I mishit the shot and in any case the lobbed header from a standing position was a far more accomplished finish. My final and 12th goal of the campaign came in the 3-3 home draw with JEB, a scissor-kick left foot shot following a corner which had bounced high across the six-yard box. Yes! The Player-of-the-Year trophy was destined to become mine at long last!

In 2002/2003 I was back in the centre of the Ely Park Rangers defence, but missed the opening day Division 2A defeat at Boathouse Rangers. We then won 2-1 at Fulbourn Institute however, and 3-1 at Barton Mills.

In our first home match of the season I put us ahead against Fen Ditton with a glancing near post header from a corner, but we were pegged back and had to settle for a 1-1 draw. We went top of the table with a 3-1 home win against Arbury, and then hammered Swaffham United Reserves 7-1 in the Preliminary Round of the Junior Cup.

Cup matches were coming thick and fast at this point – all

of them at home - and in the First Round of the Sunday League Cup, Division 1A side Jenny Wren were dispatched 5-2. In the First Round of the Millennium Cup we edged out Ickleton 4-3, but at the same stage of the Junior Cup we were thumped 5-1 by Jockey Giants. Back in the League Cup (Second Round), we defeated Trumpington Tornadoes 4-1 and in the Millennium Cup (again the Second Round) we saw off Arbury 5-3.

We resumed league action next, winning 5-1 at Wicken Maids Head as I scored with a skidding free-kick which went through the goalkeeper's legs. I was on target again the following week, stabbing home Brian Halliwell's pass in the 4-2 home win at the expense of Studlands Park. Fulbourn Institute were the next visitors to Paradise, and we kept our first clean sheet of the season in a 2-0 success.

In the Third Round of the League Cup we hammered Division 4A giant killers Newnham Rangers 7-0 to reach the last eight of the competition for the first time in the club's history. Back in the league the same scoreline sent Wicken Maids Head packing, and in the Millennium Cup quarter-final we went one better, crushing Brinkley Red Lion 8-0. Then came a league double-header against Swaffham United Reserves, with the away game resulting in a 3-0 victory and the home game resulting in a 9-0 win, earning the club the Sunday League Merit Award for January.

In the last four of the Millennium Cup we faced Fulbourn Institute, coming from behind to reach a major final for the first time in the club's history. During the tie I struck my last ever goal for Ely Park Rangers, falling backwards to sweep home Stephen Ball's cross with a cracking half-volley from the edge of the area to make it 2-2 midway through the second half. We eventually ran out 5-2 winners to earn a final clash with FC Sterling, but first of all we had to take them on in the quarter-final of the

League Cup.

The much-fancied Cambridge side had by far the better of the match and hit the bar twice, but we grabbed the only goal of the game to earn a home semi-final encounter with Senior Division leaders Alcia Athletic. The clash with FC Sterling was our 11th home cup draw out of 11 that season, which must be something of a record. In the meantime however, we had some league points to earn.

In the home clash with Boathouse Rangers we avenged our opening day defeat with a 2-0 victory, putting us nine points clear at the top of Division 2A. Our next match was against local rivals QPR Ely on 23 March 2003, and I nodded a corner back across goal for Mark Hills to make the final score 1-1. QPR's opener was the first goal we had conceded in 510 minutes, and the points we dropped were the first since 22 September 2002.

In the League Cup semi-final against Alcia we played really well and deservedly led, courtesy of a penalty kick from my namesake Steve Green (the Younger!) I was playing up front and was causing their central defender* a lot of problems, but had to go off with an Achilles tendon injury midway through the first half. The visitors eventually got back on terms, and there were no further goals so the tie went to a penalty shoot-out. Ironically, Steve Green (the younger) was the only Ely player to miss from the spot, so we lost the tie 5-4 on penalties.

> *The Alcia centre-half had played in the World Cup Qualifying Rounds. Admittedly it was for St Kitts & Nevis and they lost by double-figures to Jamaica over two legs, but at least he was there.*

My injury was serious, so I missed the next three league games – a 5-0 win at Studlands Park, a 4-1 win at Arbury and a 3-0 loss at Fen Ditton – the team's first defeat in 15 matches. When the Millennium Cup Final at Soham came along I was not 100% fit, and our opponents FC Sterling duly avenged their League Cup quarter-final defeat by an identical 1-0 margin. It was an absolutely atrocious match, but they thoroughly deserved their success on the day.

Ely Park Rangers finally clinched the Division 2A title with a 2-0 win over QPR Ely, but finished their campaign by losing at home in the league for the first time. Visiting Barton Mills grabbed the only goal of the game, and secured the runners-up berth as a result. It was only the fifth goal we had conceded at home in the league during 2002/2003, and the only time we had failed to find the net in 20 home league and cup outings, which otherwise yielded an impressive 78 goals.

CHAPTER TWENTY: The History Boys

In the First Round of the 1988/1989 Lewis Cup the Inland Revenue were drawn to play arch-rivals Customs & Excise. The fixtures were always on Wednesdays, but for some reason this game was played on a Tuesday and unfortunately for me I turned up on the wrong day! I was mortified, but nevertheless grateful to discover that we had edged through by the odd goal in five. I was back in the side for the Second Round tie against HASSRA (London South), and grabbed a hat-trick in our 5-1 victory. HASSRA (London North) were next up, and I was again on the scoresheet as we eased through by a 5-2 margin.

I was unavailable for the quarter-final trip to Plymouth to play Plymouth Civil Service, but the Inland Revenue beat them for the first time since my involvement with the team, the 3-1 victory earning us another semi-final clash with DTI (Phoenix Rovers). Once again we proved too strong for them, and I scored twice in a 4-1 success which pitched us into the final against yet another HASSRA side – this time it was North Fylde. I didn't score in the final, but a 3-1 scoreline ensured that the Lewis Cup would fall into the hands of the Inland Revenue for only the third time in 67 years.

The 1989/1990 season was the first for Porthmadog star-striker Dave Taylor, and our opponents in the First Round were MOD (Main) – a team representing the Ministry of Defence, and always very tough to beat. Attempting to retain the Lewis Cup for the first time, we got off to the best possible start. I nodded on a throw-in at the near post, and Taylor was able to mark his debut with the opening goal. I then added a second with a powerful 15-yard shot on the turn, and as the half-time whistle approached we looked totally in control. However, an under hit back-pass let in MOD to make it 2-1, and they overran us in the second period to run out 5-2 winners on the day. It was the first and only time I ever lost at the first hurdle in the Lewis Cup.

In 1990/1991 – under new manager Gwyn James – we were drawn against a very poor Department of Environment team in the First Round, and after opening the scoring with a header I eventually helped myself to six goals in a whopping 17-0 win. My sixth goal in that rout took my personal Lewis Cup tally to 50, but having been a 'favourite' of three previous National Team managers it soon became apparent that Gwyn James was not my greatest fan. I could understand this to some extent because he had the undoubted striking talents of Dave Taylor and Paul Patey at his disposal, but for me the combination of Taylor and Patey did not work as well because they were both pure goalscorers, and both rather greedy as a consequence. The Taylor/Green or Patey/Green partnerships were always more effective in my view, because I was prepared to make space and provide opportunities for them – not just for myself. And of course, more than anything I wanted to be in the starting line-up.

We went out of the 1990/1991 competition in the quarter-finals, going down by the only goal of the game against HASSRA (Midlands). In the 1991/1992 Lewis Cup we faced the same opponents again in the last eight, but this time edged them out 2-1. Out of favour now, I was substitute for the semi-final against HASSRA (Scotland) which was played at Belle Vue in Manchester. The pitch was in the middle of a high-rise council estate, and after about 20 minutes one of the HASSRA players inexplicably fell over and injured himself. We didn't know why at the time, but suddenly a huge gaping hole opened up in the pitch so we had to re-locate to a nearby school pitch (although I joked that we could have continued by placing some traffic cones around the pot-hole, which was only eight-feet deep and six-feet across). The tie resumed about an hour later, but I never got a run-out and Taylor got the only goal of the game with a superb header which bounced into the far corner of the net.

In the final at Chiswick we faced Plymouth Civil Service, and again I was named as one of the substitutes. After 20 minutes however, Paul Patey suffered an injury so I was introduced to the fray much earlier than I could have hoped for, and soon had the Plymouth defence in disarray. I struck the bar with the outside of my right foot in the first half, and at the start of the second period managed to double our 1-0 interval advantage. My first left-foot strike was parried by the goalkeeper to the left side of the penalty area, about two yards from the touchline. The 'keeper covered his near post, undoubtedly anticipating a cross. What he didn't expect was a blistering first-time left-foot shot that flew over his right shoulder and high into the net behind him. I don't think he even saw it, and I certainly don't think I ever hit a shot any harder than that in my life. The angle was so tight that most onlookers couldn't believe I had scored from that position.

Midfielder Joe Reilly put Plymouth back in the hunt with a bizarre own goal, running the ball past his own goalkeeper from the edge of the penalty area, but we were by far the better side and ran out deserving 4-2 winners.

In the season that followed (1992/1993), we again reached the final against HASSRA (North West). This time – owing to the unavailability of Dave Taylor – I was in the starting line-up alongside Paul Patey. It was extremely windy, and in the first period we had the elements in our favour, albeit against a very physical Merseyside defence who dished it out at every opportunity.

I inexplicably failed to connect when the ball flashed across the HASSRA goal in the opening minutes of the match, but midway through the first half broke the deadlock in spectacular fashion. A break down the left produced a looping cross in my direction, but the wind held the ball up ahead of me. I therefore launched myself headlong for a 15-yard diving header which flew with a slight curve into the bottom left-hand corner.

I then hit a 30-yard shot on the turn which was well saved by the goalkeeper, but in the second half my physical battering by the HASSRA defence took its toll and I limped off the pitch on the hour mark. With less than a minute remaining we still led by that solitary goal, but our replacement goalkeeper – the towering Loudon Muir – made a catastrophic error to hand our opponents a last-gasp equaliser. A bobbling, angled effort from a HASSRA striker struck the far post and then rebounded across the line towards the other post. Now Loudon was about six feet six inches tall, and had the mobility of a tanker in the Solent, so when he turned to see what was happening behind him, the ball struck his shin off the second post and deflected into the goal.

I was gutted, because HASSRA were buoyant and my goal – which should have been the only one of the game – would almost certainly be consigned to history, so I sat on the touchline and watched the extra-time drama unfold. First of all the Inland Revenue pushed forward and scored two spectacular goals to make it 3-1 at midway. Then HASSRA hit back to make it 3-3 and force a penalty shoot-out. Again I was gutted, because I would normally have been a participant in any shoot-out, but as it was the Inland Revenue prevailed 5-4 to retain the Lewis Cup for the first time in their history. My diving header was destined to become a largely forgotten detail in the context of what turned out to be a dramatic outcome to an otherwise ordinary encounter.

In 1993/1994 we again reached the final, but despite having scored 54 goals in 51 Lewis Cup appearances I was once again named as substitute. This time we faced our bitter rivals Customs & Excise, who took an early lead in their attempt to deprive us of a third successive victory in the competition. Gwyn James had me warming up on the touchline after just 20 minutes, but with 20 minutes of the match remaining I was still warming up and was still on the wrong side of the touchline. Eventually he made the decision to bring me on, and almost immediately I had the Customs defence under pressure. My goal bound shot was blocked by a defender, and we were suddenly in the ascendency. "I thought you looked a bit quick", the referee said to me shortly after my introduction, but it was all to no avail. We lost 1-0 and my career in the National Team was effectively over.

The Inland Revenue Football Club was destined never to win the Lewis Cup again.

I travelled with the team to Worcester City for a match the following season, but was substitute again and didn't get on. So that was pretty much it for me, and my final scoring record for the team read: Played 52, Goals 54. Footballers often say afterwards that they "didn't appreciate it at the time," but I have to say that I did. I relished every train journey, every match, every goal and every friendship made over 17 years. I had a whale of a time.

CHAPTER TWENTY-ONE: The Final Chapter?

I finally retired from competitive football on Saturday 4 May 2013 – the last day of the 2012/2013 season and co-incidentally, the date of my 53rd birthday. In less than a year I would undergo a triple heart by-pass operation, having been diagnosed with severe angina.

I made a 15-minute cameo appearance as substitute for the Sandy-based Sir William Peel Sunday side in Flitwick, but nearly passed out in the dressing room before the game due to the fumes emanating from the breath of my team mates! (Fortunately I strained my hamstring days later and never heard from them again!) I was subsequently speaking to my work colleague David Cullum jnr, who was playing for my former club Littleport Town. Knee problems had caused him to drop into the Reserves, and they were languishing near the foot of Premier Division B (the third tier of the County League in Cambridgeshire, in which I had previously played for Soham Town Rangers Reserves more than two decades earlier). I thought I might be able to contribute something to the club I had last played for in 1995 (i.e. make matters worse), so I duly signed up and made myself available for the next match against fellow strugglers Duxford United.

Now Duxford is not the easiest place to get to when your partner needs the car, so – in the Arctic conditions that were prevailing at the time – I attempted to re-enact the movie 'Trains, Planes and Automobiles (although in truth seeing Duxford Imperial War Museum in the distance was the nearest I got to any planes). Denise gave me a lift in the car to Hitchin. I then got a train to Cambridge, and caught another train out of Cambridge to Whittlesford. I then walked the two miles or so from Whittlesford station to Duxford. When I arrived it was sleeting, and the cramped dressing room did not help to make things any more comfortable.

Player-manager Paul Starling introduced me to the rest of the players, and then informed me that I would be starting off as one of the substitutes! So I spent the first half trying to keep warm in increasingly hostile weather conditions, occasionally running the line to stave off the imminent prospect of hypothermia.

At the interval Littleport Reserves led 2-0, but 'Starls' was not happy with the forward play so he brought me on for the second half – by which time the sleet had eased off! I soon showed that I could still head a ball at least, and began to contribute to the general play by linking with the midfield (and with David Cullum jnr in particular, who was Littleport's outstanding player by far). We went 3-0 up when I made a run behind the Duxford defence on the right side of the penalty area, and David clipped the ball forward into my path. Instead of crossing it into the six-yard box, I angled the ball backwards towards Dave Cornwell, who was left with the simple task of steering his shot into the far corner of the net.

I subsequently made an almost identical run to create a chance for myself, but a covering defender just got back in time to get a toe-end on my goal bound effort and the opportunity was lost. Duxford managed to pull a goal back at this stage, but Cullum made the points safe with a direct free-kick which made the final score 4-1 to us.

I tweaked my hamstring again just before the final whistle, so I was unavailable for the 2-0 home defeat at the hands of West Wratting Reserves. My next match was at Bluntisham Rangers on a very poor pitch, and although I put myself about (stretching the material of one defender's shirt to a world-record length) we were beaten 3-0. The following Saturday it was Bluntisham again, but I couldn't make it and 'Port won that one by the odd goal in five.

Then came the visit to West Row Gunners, managed by my ex-Ely City team-mate David Lowe, who coincidentally had been in the Tuddenham Rovers line-up when I played my solitary game for them at Gransden Chequers a few years earlier. The weather was even worse than it had been at Duxford, but thankfully the pitch was in good condition and we played really well in the first half. David Cullum jnr gave us the lead, and I was involved in the move which gave us a two-goal advantage. Unfortunately my hamstring gave way again in the freezing conditions, so I had no alternative but to come off at half-time. West Row were not very good in my opinion, but two second half penalties helped them to claim a 3-2 victory they barely deserved.

The hamstring problem meant that I missed the 1-1 draw at Hardwick Reserves, but I was available again for the home clash with Duxford, although I started the match as substitute. We trailed 1-0 at the break, so 'Starls' brought me on and before long we were awarded a penalty. I volunteered to take it, and did what I always did – looked to the left and fired it to the right. The penalty was perfect, but my hamstring was not and as soon as I struck the ball I felt a twinge in the back of my thigh. So instead of jogging back into my own half for the kick-off, I limped sideways off the pitch like a crippled crab and back to the dressing room! We lost 2-1.

In my subsequent absence, Littleport beat Longstanton 4-2 at home before going down 2-0 at home to top-of-the-table Gamlingay United. The midweek return match with Gamlingay was next on the agenda, and I was very keen to play because it gave me the opportunity to play against Denise's 17-year old son Nathan. I lasted just over an hour and played mainly in a defensive role, and although Nathan thankfully didn't manage to score, a late goal meant that my home village secured all three points. Some of the village spectators had given me rather odd looks when I ran on to the field that evening in the green of Littleport Town!

I missed the visit to eventual runners-up Comberton United which resulted in a 3-2 defeat, but I was back for the trip to Hemingfords United Reserves when I had perhaps my best game in a 4-0 win. I was again absent when Littleport Reserves suffered yet another 3-2 loss – this time at Longstanton – so we approached the final game of the season needing at least a point to avoid relegation*.

> *Because we knew that in all probability we would forfeit three points for fielding an ineligible player earlier in the season.*

We gave a good account of ourselves against Comberton, but two own goals condemned us to a 2-0 defeat in a match where we seldom threatened to score. I didn't see a lot of the ball, but at least I never once gave it away. In the first half I hit their centre-half, and he just looked at me and said "Fucking hell, how old are you?" I responded by saying "Old enough, sonny!" So that was it. Seven appearances and not a single goal in open play...

Later that year – after I had been diagnosed with severe angina – I travelled with David Cullum jnr to Leeds University to play for Eastern Counties in the annual Veterans Competition. My first experience of Veterans football in the Civil Service though, had been for the England team at Portsmouth University in 2009, when we faced teams from Wales, Scotland, Northern Ireland and the Republic of Ireland. We beat Wales 1-0 in our first game, but then drew all our remaining games to hand Scotland the title.

In 2010 the tournament was held at Waterford in the Republic of Ireland, and again we won our first match 1-0

– this time at the expense of Scotland. Unfortunately we again drew all our remaining games, so on this occasion it was the Republic who ended up as champions. After 2010 it was decided that England should be divided up into regions to give more veterans the opportunity to play in the competition, so in 2011 I represented Eastern Counties at Largs in Scotland.

We lost our opening game 2-0 to Newcastle Estates, and then drew 0-0 with Wales when I was unlucky not to score with a header that hit the underside of the bar. We therefore played off against South Region and South East Region for the dubious honour of finishing ninth, and I suddenly found my scoring touch again – or rather my genitals did, as a cross-ball drifted over the goalkeeper and into my nether regions before nestling in the back of the net.

In the final game against South East however, I was once again 'in the zone'. The 'keeper was down at his near post when a pass reached me just outside the six-yard box, but I was faced by two defenders. I therefore knocked the ball about a yard to the right, and then angled my shot between the two of them to open the scoring.

Soon afterwards I was on target again, turning sharply on the edge of the penalty box before drifting a shot into the top right-hand corner. Then I completed my hat-trick, moving towards a right wing cross before planting a downward header past the flat-footed goalkeeper. Our opponents pulled one back before the interval, but I grabbed my fourth goal in the second half, this time heading home a cross which took a skidding bounce before reaching me. We eventually won that match 5-1.

Having scored five goals as a 51-year old in that tournament, I was looking forward to the 2012 competition at Bisham Abbey. We beat North Region 2-1 in our opening game, but could only draw 1-1 with Newcastle Estates so they qualified for the semi-finals at our expense. We then crashed 5-0 against Yorkshire before concluding our efforts with a 3-0 win against Wales. I came on as substitute in this one, and when we were awarded a free-kick on the edge of the penalty area the Wales goalkeeper was holding on to the left-hand post, positioning his wall. As the wall gradually retreated, I asked the referee if I could take the free-kick straight away. He confirmed that I could, so with the goalkeeper still on his post I simply curled the ball into the opposite corner! The Welsh players were not at all happy! Then again, happiness is not something that necessarily comes naturally for the Welsh…

So in 2013 we were at Leeds University, when I have to say we played some terrific football. Unfortunately however, we did not have a goalkeeper to speak of. So despite outplaying Scotland in our opener and taking a 1-0 lead, we lost 2-1. Afterwards, one of the Scotland players said that they could see no way back into the game. "We just couldn't get the ball off you!" he said.

Our 'invisible' goalkeeper then let in another goal as we lost 1-0 to Manchester despite completely outplaying them, so that meant we were playing off for ninth place at best. In the afternoon we beat the Republic of Ireland 1-0, and I was responsible for the only goal from the penalty spot. I adopted my usual technique – looking to the left and striking to the right – but just before I connected I noticed that the goalkeeper was diving to the right as well (i.e. to his left). So at the last second, I adjusted my footing and scuffed the ball to the middle of the goal instead. It bobbled into the net past the 'keeper's foot, but my team-mates came to the conclusion that it was a shit penalty and that I had been lucky to score! I tried to explain to them that what I had done was in fact an act of pure genius, but they were having none of it and took the piss for the remainder of the trip.

I missed the 2014 trip to Brunel University in London because I was recuperating from my heart operation, but returned for the competition at Lilleshall the following year at the age of 55. I thought I did OK but in three matches against East Midlands, North West (the eventual winners) and Scotland (the eventual runners-up) we failed to score a goal.

In late 2014 I had resumed training with the Gamlingay lads, and in the second session I experienced another one of those 'special' moments. Nathan's best friend Joseph Webb laid the ball back to me, and I hit a first-time right-foot shot from 15-yards (which is quite a way out in six-a-side matches). It flew into the top left-hand corner of the net, and I said afterwards that I had not hit a shot as sweetly as that for 25 years. Mind you, on the other side of the coin Ashley Dean had nutmegged me about five times during the same session.

When I left the pub, I asked the lads not to take the piss out of me as soon as I had gone. Ben Eadie therefore suggested that I should stay a little longer, because they were just about to start... Don't worry Ben. I intend to be around for a while yet.